THE
SMALL GARDEN
PLANNER

THE
SMALL GARDEN
PLANNER

GRAHAM ROSE

A Fireside Book
Published by Simon & Schuster Inc.
New York London Toronto Sydney Tokyo Singapore

FIRESIDE
Simon & Schuster Building
Rockefeller Center
1230 Avenue of the Americas
New York, New York 10020

FIRESIDE and colophon are registered trademarks
of Simon & Schuster Inc.

Published in Great Britain
by Mitchell Beazley Publishers
Edited and designed by Mitchell Beazley International Ltd,
Artists House, 14-15 Manette Street, London SW1V 5LB

Design Zöe Davenport
Editor Zuza Vrbova
Botanical Consultant Sabina Knees
Illustrations Pam Williams
Production Peter Phillips

Library of Congress Cataloging in Publication Data

Rose, Graham
     The small garden planner.

     Includes index.
     1. Gardens——Designs.   2. Landscape gardening.
     3. Gardens——Pictorial works.   1. Title
SB473.R593 1987   712'.6   87–16304

ISBN 0–671–72408–8

The publishers have made every effort to ensure that all instructions given
in this book are accurate and safe, but they cannot accept liability for any
resulting injury, damage or loss to either person or property whether
direct or consequential and howsoever arising. The author and publishers
will be grateful for any information which will assist them in keeping future
editions up to date.

Typeset Vantage Photosetting Ltd., Eastleigh and London.
Color reproduction by Colourscan, Singapore
Printed in Italy by L.E.G.O., Vicenza

10 9 8 7 6 5 4 3 2 1

Note
Numbers within brackets in the photograph captions in this
book refer to features that are identified on the relevant plan.
The symbol ● is used to highlight points of general information
or advice.

AMERICAN EDITOR: FAYAL GREENE

CONTENTS

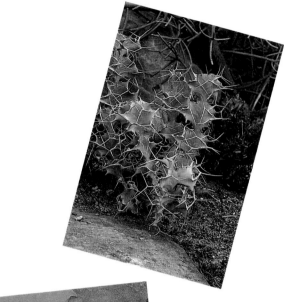

TAKING A FRESH LOOK

How much simpler it would be to plan a small garden if we could photograph the future and study the end result before we laid a brick or planted a shrub. A degree of vision is required in creating gardens of any size, but when you are working with a small area the need for forethought becomes even more important because you are usually shaping a view which is close at hand, and early mistakes may be hard to rectify.

As few of us have the gift of precognition, the next best thing is to look at other people's gardens and learn from them. In this book you will find designs for widely-differing small gardens. The photographs will inspire you as you recognize similarities to your own situation. The plans are not meant to be rigid prescriptions—rather, each represents one solution to the problems inherent in designing for small spaces. The selections of plants, paving and walling materials can all be adapted to suit your own region, needs and tastes. If you particularly like the shape or color of a plant which is not suitable or available in your area, you should be able to find substitutes which give the same effect by consulting a knowledgeable nursery. The catalogs and magazines listed in the back of the book will also prove helpful.

Although individual needs vary widely, a common desire is to achieve a sense of seclusion, calm and intimacy, and to create views from both the house and garden that please the eye.

A first principle is to think carefully about scale. No matter how tiny and constricted the plot, when looking at or sitting in it we like to entertain the notion that it is boundless. This kind of self-deception is difficult to bring off unless the scale of the plants and the other elements of the garden are related to the size of the plot and its surroundings. Building fences higher than the width of the lot, for example, may achieve seclusion only at the cost of creating an unpleasant corridor effect.

If you have moved into a house with an existing but unappealing garden, it is sensible to live with it for a time before destroying it to start again. You may be able to incorporate some already mature plants in the new plan. Although impatience is understandable, try to resist introducing poor-quality structural materials even if it means waiting until you can afford something better. One of the advantages of smallness is that you need not invest in large quantities of plants, materials or ornaments and can choose the more exquisite plants and the more expensive natural materials rather than cheaper substitutes. This can give small gardens a feeling of quality that many larger gardens lack.

ASSEMBLING THE FEATURES

The great joy in gardening is that it offers the individual almost perfect liberty. However, without a controlled plan of approach, a garden can easily grow into chaos rather than an idyllic jungle. The details of the finest informal-looking gardens have usually been carefully thought through, right down to the placement of the last miniature narcissus bulb. A precise site plan on graph paper is an

The door of the house warrants careful attention, to make it welcoming. In this tiny front garden, a laburnum and yellow rose are balanced by another rose overhanging ground-level window boxes. The window grille is reminiscent of a trellis.

invaluable aid in the initial planning stages. The garden boundaries and any existing features you want to retain—walls, doorways, terracing or pathways—should all be marked on first. Then the position of mature trees and the extent of foliage of any long-established plants you want to keep should be plotted. Trees and shrubs that conflict with the new plan for the garden can sometimes be retained with judicious pruning.

Once the master site plan is complete, it should never be further marked. Any changes and additions to the plan should be made either on a transparent overlay of tracing paper or on photocopies of the original. This will enable the impact of any changes on the whole design to be judged, in the context of the fundamental plan.

The ideal location for permanent features such as changes of level, paths, seats, water features and trellis screens should be established and marked on the plan before considering the most suitable locations for the slightly more versatile elements such as pergolas, obelisks and planting posts.

Experience dictates that there is little point in being too subtle and optimistic in one's approach to planning the paths, because people tend to take the straightest route from one point to another in a garden. If you do not want paths to follow direct lines along these routes, it may be advisable to make sure that the structure of walls or planting along winding paths is positive enough to keep people's footsteps on the right track. As a wide path tends to rob small gardens of valuable planting space, I recommend a maximum width of a mere 15in (40cm). However, I would not want to be too dogmatic about either of these points. Many of the gardens illustrated in this book show that rules can be broken with fruitful effect.

Although pathways on the plan may appear to be rather obtrusive, they need not be so in practice. Plants can be allowed to partially impinge on areas dedicated to walkways, whether they are simply soft gravel tracks or hard paving; alternatively, small mound-forming plants can be deliberately positioned in the gaps between paving stones to make the surface seem softer and more interesting.

SURROUNDS

The boundaries of the garden and the walls of the house are usually the most important features in a small garden, and unless a design copes with them successfully, the overall plan is bound to fail. The ideal is to create the impression that the house walls themselves have been built deliberately as part of a beautiful integrated scheme in which sympathetic materials have been used throughout. By looking at the house wall visible from the garden as if it is part of the garden, you may be able to make some worthwhile visual changes, for example by adding shutters in order to "spread" windows or by modifying the style of doors and windows.

Provided that the brick, stone, shingle or chipboard of the house wall is beautiful, you may want to leave large areas of it exposed, although most materials are usually improved by "softening" with some vegetation.

Characterless walls can be enhanced by attaching trellis panels to them. Fortunately, there are many choices of creepers and climbing plants which will flourish on walls of any aspect and rapidly mask and enrich the appearance of nondescript walling materials. For example, the small-leaved Virginia creeper (*Parthenocissus tricuspidata*) and *Clematis montana* prosper even on difficult north-facing walls. *Hydrangea petiolaris*

Top **Stone walls** provide a backdrop for raised planting.

Above **Pots** crammed with color enliven dull architectural features.

or, in Southern regions, the common white jasmine (*Jasminum officinale*) do well on east walls. Options are even greater for warmer south and west walls; plants like the bell-flowered scarlet *Campsis radicans* bring a touch of the tropics to virtually any climate, while in truly sub-tropical areas the fragrant white-flowered evergreen *Trachelospermum jasminoides* is spectacular in every way.

Unattractive garden perimeter walls can usually be hidden completely behind a solid evergreen mattress. Good covering plants are cotoneaster, evergreen viburnum and, of course, the various sorts of ivy. *Ceanothus* and *Fremontodendron californicum* bring glamor to the surroundings of those lucky enough to be able to grow them.

Rather rather than simply substituting the hard features of the original wall with an unbroken green curtain, which will still leave the boundaries fairly evident, an effective tactic is to plant free-standing tall evergreen shrubs or trees in front of a creeper-clad wall. Intermittently seen through the branches of a graceful evergreen, the wall cladding will appear to be simply the enticing green shadow beneath the canopy of an endless woodland. Good choices of evergreens might be Cripps' Hinoki cypress (*Chamaecyparis obtusa crippsii*), Korean pine (*Pinus koraiensis*, holly (*Ilex* × *altaclerensis*) or columnar Japanese yew (*Taxus* × *media* 'Hicksii').

The need to make the boundary disappear is greatest in properties built of poor-quality materials such as cement-based blocks. On the other hand, well-established walls of handsome brick, mellow stone, or well-made wooden fencing can blend beautifully with plants. Interesting features such as fine moldings or changes of plane may be left exposed, or decorative additions of sculpture, basins or fountains may be made. A good-quality wall

enhanced by the freckle of flowers or subtle foliage will create a splendid, though obviously confined, garden, in which the feeling of secret calm is ample substitute for wider vistas.

An important role of a perimeter wall in a small garden can be its ability to mask undesirable views of surrounding buildings. Nothing so destroys the idyllic private feeling of a beautiful garden than a glimpse of the neighbor's plastic-roofed car port or the bedroom windows of the house beyond the end wall, which appear to pry into your private space. In more rural surroundings, perimeter masking may be equally effective in creating shelter for delicate plants and providing a comfortable homestead feeling.

If the object is to mask an unwanted view, simply raising the height of a wall as little as two or three feet often suffices. Bear in mind, however, the danger of making a very small garden feel claustrophobic by building solid walls too high. An inexpensive and easy alternative is to attach wooden columns to the walls, providing supports for trellising. Even while still bare, the pattern of the trellis itself will do much to convey privacy, and plants such as the honeysuckle or ivy will scramble up the trellis quickly. Before deciding to increase the height of the perimeter wall or fence, it pays to carefully examine the existing environment to see if the offending view cannot be more attractively masked by small trees or large shrubs placed in the line of sight.

The surroundings of a small garden are not always unappealing. By studying the landscape and buildings beyond your own lot you may see opportunities to open a "window" onto some charming view by selective pruning of established trees on your own lot or by reducing the height of your boundary wall or fence in particular places and increasing its height in others.

Top **Trellis work** may be painted white for emphasis, but when the planting is colorful you may prefer the wood in its natural state.

Above **Instead of obscuring** the next plot with a wall or solid fence, you can use trelliswork to combine seclusion with openness.

Top **Combining** two paving surfaces—such as brick and stone—adds interest to a plot.

Above **Timber decking** is expensive, but you can confine it to a path between beds.

In a well-planned small garden, the walls or fences themselves can compensate for lack of planting space on the ground. Their strong vertical dimension provides wonderful opportunities to enrich the garden with a host of climbers that only need sheltered support to prosper. Lower walls within the garden can be used to create partially enclosed areas for spatial variety and increase plant density by providing support for plants set in holes pierced in their sides or planted in troughs along their tops.

Hedges, although not as effective as masonry in reducing noise, are another means of preserving a garden's sense of intimacy, especially if they are evergreen, tall and dense. Closely planted pyracantha, box, yew or *Thuja* make good surrounds in cool, temperate gardens, while griselinia, cypresses, escallonia and olearia are good hedging subjects in warmer climates.

All these plants tolerate frequent clipping which promotes thick lower growth and helps to prevent gaps appearing in the hedge. They are best planted in two lines, 1½ft (45cm) apart at intervals of 3ft (90cm) in the row, set so that the plants in one row are stationed in the center of the gap between the plants in the other row.

PAVINGS AND PATHS

Paving is the "hardscape" of the garden—the hard surfaces that provide a useful foil to the foliage "upholstery".

If only to avoid earth being tramped into the house, most small gardens need some form of dry terrace to mediate between the planted areas of the garden and the doors leading out to it. If you want to use the terrace for entertaining, an area of only 64 sq ft (6 sq m) will provide adequate dry seating for a group of eight people and an additional hard standing area of 8ft × 6ft (2.5m × 2m) should provide a sufficient base for a barbecue, with room for it to be attended. An irregular shape is often more interesting than a simple rectangle, provided that it does not become overfussy in design. The function of the terrace should be given due weight in planning its placement and shape.

The need to use materials which harmonize well with the general environment is as important when selecting surfaces at ground level as it is in making decisions about walling. Until ground areas are softened and partly hidden by plant foliage, they will be very obvious features in a small garden.

The material used for the topping of all hard standing areas, and surrounding the planted areas of soil, must be considered at the same time as the walling is selected. Paving, in particular, is an important purchase and it makes sense to test its suitability on site by buying a sample and taking it home to match against the color and character of the existing walls. Quarried stone is the most luxurious choice. Avoid the cheapest stone substitutes, as they may begin to flake within a few years.

The effects of weather on topping material need to be gauged when selecting paving or aggregates from the wide variety now available. Some stones and aggregates are depressing when wet, or are drab in bright sunlight; however, there are gravels which glow a mild pink when dry and flush to a warm red when wet. Paving is particularly susceptible to damage by frost or blazing sunshine, and no matter which material is chosen it should be laid on a well-compacted base. Hard materials of large dimension can simply and easily be laid on compacted soil, topped with sand. But small units such as bricks or tiles need a "float" of

Top **Mound-forming plants** in gaps left in a paved terrace look effective when they spill over the edges.

Above **Brick "islands"** are useful to break the monotony of a sea of gravel. Sculptural logs complete the picture.

concrete or compacted hard core to make a base on which they are unlikely to subside. The depth of base necessary will depend on how cold the area gets in winter.

There are occasions when a bright or a highly decorative topping might fit perfectly into the overall design, but, particularly in winter, when deciduous plants have either dropped their leaves or died back, the terraced parts of the garden are very conspicuous and you may not wish them to become too dominant. A good general rule is to confine spectacular topping to rather small and well-bounded areas where less assertive materials frame it. In most successful small gardens the paving is fairly neutral, leaving the plants to command the most attention. Some types of reconstituted stone paving imitate stone fairly convincingly but the illusion will be spoiled if cracks appear, so lay it with care—it is easily broken. Although they are somewhat harder to lay, paving units of smaller dimensions are more appropriate in small gardens than large slabs.

AGGREGATES

There is a wonderful variety of gravels, ground rock and coarse grits available that make most successful yet economical pavements. These aggregates come in all shapes, sizes and colors. They drain and dry out as quickly as solid paving and because they refract light, they tend to soften the appearance of the whole garden. Some can simply be spread over the complete ground surface, including the planted areas. If aggregates are used to top the well-defined areas, such as patios, terraces or paths, they should ideally be kept in place between hard edges such as mortared bricks, cut stone or timber boards.

Plants grow well through loose materials, so before spreading aggregates, the soil should be topped with a layer of black sheet polyethylene to prevent weed germination. This will also prevent the aggregate from being trodden into the soil below in wet weather. To ensure good drainage, puncture the plastic at intervals with the prongs of a hand fork.

Increasingly, a range of interesting and useful "ready to lay" aggregate materials is becoming available. The stone element is bound in a resin which is soft when first exposed and easy to lay but hardens in contact with the air, to provide a very durable surface. These aggregates can be obtained in a variety of colors which makes it possible to form geometric or abstract patterns or to use them in combination with more traditional paving materials such as stone, brick or concrete.

WOOD

Wood has a wonderful natural quality which always marries beautifully with vegetation and can be exploited to great advantage in any garden. It is especially effective for surfacing terraces in gardens of houses that use wood as a predominant feature of their construction. The traditional redwood or cedar planking on a supported frame provides an ideal formal terrace.

Alternatively, horizontal sections cut through tree trunks can create useful steps over soft ground and in lawns, or can provide visual variety when clustered together and set flush with an aggregate surface. All wood used in the garden should be thoroughly treated with preservatives to prevent decay due to fungal and insect attack.

The use of ground or shredded tree bark to top paths and planted areas has been so widely adopted recently that it has become a gardening cliché. However, it does act as a slow humus provider and a moisture-retaining weed-suppressing mulch. The more attractive grades can make a good ground topping, especially if you want to create a woodland effect. If bark is used, you will need to add a higher than normal annual dressing of nitrogenous fertilizer to planted beds, to compensate for nitrogen used by bacteria which slowly transform the bark into humus.

LAWNS
Botanically, it is much more rewarding to pack a small area with beautiful and interesting plants than to create a lawn. In a small garden the lawn tends to be heavily used, continually suffering from treading and compacting and this usually produces a scarred, patchy effect radically different from the velvety emerald sward displayed on seed and fertilizer packets. My own advice would be against including a conventional lawn in the plan for any small garden. To achieve a smooth palette of green as a counterpoint to the fussiness of shrubs and flowering plants, an alternative strategy is to be very deliberate and create a microlawn—a specially raised rectangular trough. Construct the trough by building walls of brick or stone 1½ft (45cm) high, 6½ft (2m) long and 2ft (60cm) wide. After pouring 10in (25cm) of compacted hardcore or gravel into the bottom of the trough, top it up with good loam and either sow lawn seed or lay pre-cut turf.

One or several such raised microlawns can be located in sunny sites in the garden and used in the overall design like any other bulky artifacts. Holes in the walls supporting the microlawns are useful for drainage or to hold trailing plants for additional interest. Microlawns introduce an interesting change into the levels of the garden and are easy to keep neat and tidy. As an alternative to lawn grass, they can be planted up with green or gold miniature thymes, *Thymus minimus* and *Thymus aureus*. These emit a wonderful heady

fragrance, flower in season and tolerate crushing. Chamomile combines scent with a lovely feathery texture. At soil level, small-leaved low-growing ground cover plants such as the lesser periwinkle (*Vinca minor*), New Zealand burr (*Acaena microphylla*) and *Ajuga reptans* also make an admirable substitute for a conventional lawn.

WATER
By its capacity to reflect the color and changing moods of the sky, water can introduce excitingly different visual experiences into a garden. When allowed to fall or cascade, the sound of water can become a soothing and therapeutic component of the natural world. The presence of a water feature also makes it possible to bring plants of a different character into the garden—no land plant offers quite the same enchanting qualities as a water lily trembling on a surface, rippled by the stealthy passage of a fish.

The magical effects of water can be introduced into even tiny gardens by making mini-ponds. A pond as small as a deep wash basin will provide sufficient water to allow a water lily to thrive or a pair of goldfish to swim. The plastic lining of some commercially-produced ponds can easily be masked by sinking it into the ground. Or, a brick or stone wall can be erected around it, with soil used to fill the gap in between, making potential planting space for trailing or small mound-forming plants. As with any water feature, an important caveat is that you must be prepared to do a good deal of light maintenance work, and this is particularly necessary if you have small, still ponds which will become stagnant unless they are kept clean. In cold areas, small ponds will need to be emptied in winter.

The reflective surface of water attracts the eye, making it possible to create beckoning

Top **Water lilies** thrive in a conventional pond or a barrel sunk into the earth. Miniature hybrids are available.

Above **The horizontal lines** of a pool should normally be offset by plants with a strongly vertical appearance.

vistas which create the illusion of a larger garden. This can be accomplished by building narrow canals of only 1½ft (45cm) in width which, even if they are only 6in (15cm) deep, will provide sufficient root space for many attractive aquatic plants.

Such canals can link small ponds, alter direction and, if connected by dams, change levels. The non-aquatic planting areas can be confined to the bases of the perimeter walls, gaps in terracing and dry islands between ponds and canals. Canal-side paths, low bridges or stepping stones will provide circulation in water gardens of this kind.

Gushing waterfalls are rarely convincing in small gardens and the sound of their splashing can become irritatingly dominant. But, the gentle splash of small quantities of water, tumbling back from a single plume fountain into a pond, or the gradual trickle of water from a wall jet into a basin, can be very pleasing and introduce a feeling of casual animation to the garden.

PERGOLAS AND TRELLISES

Just as planners of small gardens must make the best use of perimeter walls and the ground to support plants, they must also seek opportunities to intensify the effect of planting by using the air space above the garden. Trellis screens, obelisks or pergola tunnels up or over which plants can climb make gardens appear larger because they create patterns that cannot easily be understood and taken in at a brief glance. One way to sustain such interest is to partially screen areas with climbers on trellis work, which allow just enough of a glimpse of spaces beyond to intrigue the inquisitive.

When the climbers on a pergola are well-grown, forming an almost solid roof of foliage and making the sides into an intriguingly

broken screen, passing through the shade of a pergola from one section of garden to another can be an enchanting experience, as the whole environment momentarily changes. The quality of the light is different, the air is stiller and more fragrant and even sounds which are more strident in the open garden are subtly baffled. On emerging into the open garden again, it seems to offer a new set of stimuli. Pergolas are particularly useful in softening the transition between the garden and the terracing around the house.

The air can also be used to provide room for plants by making them climb up simple posts or cane tripods, whose feet are set in what is otherwise densely planted ground. Although rather stark initially, posts and tripods soon take on the allure of leafy totems as quickly-growing climbers, such as *Clematis*, begin their rampant coverage.

Planting posts, or the upright timber columns supporting trellising or a pergola, can be held erect if inserted into metal fence post bases, driven into the ground. These have the advantage that they hold the wood clear of the soil and prevent it from rotting. Wooden uprights can be firmly attached to existing masonry walls using heavy-duty expanding wall plugs. For a free-standing pergola, 2in × 4in (5cm × 10cm) rough wood can be used to make the horizontal bars which join the tops of the posts along each side of the structure and 1in × 5in (2.5cm × 12cm) planking to make the upper members, connecting the posts across the line of the pergola path. Other useful materials to support plants include wrought iron, wire mesh, wire, rope and appropriate mixtures of brick and wood. Ready-made trellis paneling is commercially available or can easily be handmade using 1in (2½cm) square roughly cut wood.

ILLUSIONS OF SPACE

Just as a pergola can alter our perception of a garden's size, so other visual devices can trick the eye. One way of making a small garden seem larger is to create different levels, linked by ramps or steps which offer an element of surprise and may help to create sheltered environments to suit a larger variety of plants. Any such changes in level should be noted carefully on the site plan before any earth moving begins.

More deliberate *trompe l'oeil* effects include the use of false-perspective treillage which can seem to create alcoves in walls, and the placement of mirrors to reflect back intriguing views. In one of the most impressive small gardens I have seen, a small stream seemed to lead from a little pond out of the garden through a low arch in its wall and meander on between flowers toward another pond. In fact, the arch was merely an arch-shaped arrangement of bricks protruding from the perimeter wall surface, confining an area of outdoor-grade mirror. Its reflected plants and water gave the impression that the garden flowed with the water beyond the wall. (A similar effect is shown on pages 82–3.)

Another ploy is to set a wrought-iron gate in a specially-built deep alcove in the end wall of the garden. If the alcove is deep enough and the gate is set across its opening, a few plants grown between the gate and the wall will evoke a sense of a second garden beyond the main one. Coupled with a heavy-gauge mirror backing to the apparent doorway, this trick seems to effectively double the length of the lot. Some art is needed to mask the edges of inset mirrors, either with foliage or trellis work, to provide a frame for the illusion. If such measures appear too elaborate, the simple act of white-washing a dull boundary fence will lighten and brighten a small garden.

ORNAMENTAL FEATURES

Style and scale are the two major factors in the selection of urns, planters, fountains or sculpture for small gardens. Such ornamental features can provide an effective key to the whole garden, but only if quality is put before quantity and proportion before pretentiousness. Too many majestic urns and planting troughs of the kind seen in great gardens such as Versailles merely look ludicrous in the average town garden.

The rule when selecting urns or planters is to pick a few good pieces of fairly simple design which conform in scale with the other elements in the garden. Stone or simulated stone reproductions of 18th-century vases, urns and troughs will beautifully garnish gardens with stone walls or paving, and terracotta versions always blend in well, especially when backed by foliage. However, they are only suitable for frost-free regions—otherwise, they must be brought inside in the cold months.

To save space, small, wall-mounted fountains should be selected rather than free-standing ones, although the latter can be worked in to an overall design as an eye-catcher.

When choosing sculptures, there is no need to shun the world of classical mythology, but on the whole it is better to be content with lissom wood nymphs or shepherds than to choose more emphatic and challenging pieces. Michelangelo's David would look altogether too much like Goliath in a small garden, and his heroic stance absurd. However, the Neptune garden on this page (top right) shows how such rules can be broken to great effect.

Top **Pots** should be of high quality, but need not be elaborately ornamental. Terracotta will look good anywhere, but check that it is frost-proof.

Above **A stone trough** for alpines and other small plants can be effectively raised on pillars of brick. In this example, note the rounded ends.

Top **Breaking the rules** can pay dividends. This Neptune fountain works well in a small garden, despite its challenging scale, which calls for bold planting.

Above, middle **Simple contrasts** of form and color usually succeed.

Above **White sculpture** instantly draws the eye.

ROOF GARDENS

The most simple roof gardens invariably succeed because of their unusual and exhilarating vistas. This means that even a sparsely planted rooftop will appear attractive. Such gardens are wonderful assets in urban areas where no other planting facility exists.

A roof garden is much easier to create if it is planned as an inherent part of a new building. Inevitably, considerable structural precautions are necessary if heavy features such as ponds and raised beds are to be supported on an existing building.

If there is any doubt about the structural strength of a roof, by far the best place to concentrate the load is directly on top of the outside wall in planters, and round its periphery in pots. Unless you have a large area of roof which will bear the heavy weight of wet soil, masonry and flooring, the plants should be housed in lightweight containers.

The surface of a roof garden can often look flat and uniform and so it is a good idea to either use a variety of paving materials or create a pattern.

Once a roof garden has been established, it will hardly differ from any other small garden. Most roof gardens are exposed to the elements and so need strong screens to provide shelter, especially from the wind. A partial screen is generally preferable to a solid screen because it is less likely to be damaged by turbulence.

Exposure to wind means that excessive evaporation can be a problem and so roof plants need frequent watering. Evaporation on a roof is also more acute than in a ground-level garden because the depth of the soil is limited and there is no contact between the topsoil and a deep subsoil moisture reservoir.

THE UTILITARIAN ACCESSORIES

Garden sheds or even utilitarian greenhouses occupy an excessive amount of space in small gardens and are so visually dominant that they tend to destroy any of the sense of magic which a good garden should try to create. A practical alternative to a shed for the storage of tools is a horizontal storage box in attractive timber, which can be stationed somewhere in the garden as a seat. A similar option is to design a shallow cupboard along a wall of the house blending with the facade.

Gardeners who want greenhouse space should consider the attractions of a small conservatory which can make a graceful addition to the charm of any garden. One option is to create a small "bay" window of pretty design, cantilevered out from the house wall above ground level. The other is to build a lean-to conservatory at ground level. Ideally, conservatories are designed as integral parts of the house, with access from one of the rooms.

SEATS AND TABLES

Psychology has a role to play in the planning of seats for small gardens and this tends to narrow the range of options. As few of us feel comfortable sitting in the middle of an open space, fixed seating usually needs to be sited either along walls or within cosy bowers formed by planting. And as a seat should encourage people to sit and talk it needs to be a sufficiently large object to accommodate two. This means that in winter, when all the leaves of the deciduous plants have vanished, it will become a rather outstanding feature. Accordingly, a modest seat with simple lines in muted tones—plain wood, dull greens and browns—is usually best.

Seats formed as integral parts of boundary walls in the same stone or brick also work well, and some of the most satisfactory seats are the simplest—large railroad ties or stone blocks fixed against a wall. Try to position any seating to offer the most pleasing and attractive view of the garden. For portable seating, avoid using plastic seats which inevitably introduce an undesirable synthetic element to the garden, and choose the plainest covering materials you can find for folding seats, which have the advantage that they can be stacked away easily in wet weather.

A table is one of the most useful pieces of furniture in the garden. If you use a barbecue, it is convenient to have somewhere to rest the food, as well as a table for eating. One handsome sort of table consists of a substantial stone slab permanently set on stone pillars or

Seating should be chosen either for good looks or for unobtrusive comfort.

These wicker chairs have a worn, lived-in look acceptable in an informal patio.

on sturdy wooden legs. Such a table, of course, is too heavy to move and forms an integral part of the garden design. Alternatively, many fine tables of teak or other woods, as well as metal-and-glass designs, are widely available. These have the advantage of being movable and can be stored away for the winter, if desired.

Mundane-looking but strong kitchen tables can be converted into ornamental garden tables by decorating them with tiles, fragments of stone or marble set in cement.

LIGHTING

The charm of a garden at night can be ruined by glare. The golden rule for successfully illuminating garden plants is to use white light and always direct it up into the foliage and away from the house and paths around the garden. Since the electric cable may need burying, the garden should be wired before any serious planting begins. Spiked spotlights are available which can be fixed into a bed or lawn and perhaps moved around the garden to highlight plants as they come into flower at different seasons. Spotlights with clamps are also on the market for attachment to tree branches.

PLANTING

In a small garden, mixed planting with small trees and shrubs mingled with herbaceous plants is more appealing than the classical herbaceous border which demands plenty of space. However, the classical rules of planting apply to such mixed beds, with the larger plants being stationed behind the smaller ones, the sun-lovers placed to obtain as much light as possible and the shade-lovers located where the overhead canopy or the shadow of the larger plants is likely to be densest.

For perimeter walls, the broader-leaved climbers provide good cover. If varieties with more finely divided leaves are chosen, they should be those whose habit is to produce very dense foliage. In both cases, climbers with non-variegated leaves of low tone—mid-green or darker—are most suitable because, as every interior decorator knows, dark walls are less obvious and less visually limiting than those of a brighter hue.

Plants such as ivy, Virginia creeper or clematis make excellent wall covering for high walls. The choice is limitless for lower walls because many dark evergreen shrubs, such as cotoneaster and pyracantha (firethorn) are suitable for wall training. For pergolas, silver lace vine (*Polygonum Aubertii*), grapevine, wisteria or, in warm climates, the densely dissected foliage of the passion flower (*Passiflora caerulea*) are all good choices if you want heavy coverage.

Creating foliage screens helps to give small gardens a feeling of greater depth. Hence, trees and shrubs set in from the margins of the garden should, ideally, have deep-cut, fairly loose foliage, offering glimpses of the plants beyond them. Trees such as the European weeping ash (*Fraxinus excelsior* 'Aurea Pendula'), weeping silver pear (*Pyrus salcifolia*) or honey locust (*Robinia pseudoacacia*)—or a shrub like the golden European elder (*Sambucus racemosa* 'Plumosa Aurea')—possess this characteristic. Plants with light-colored or variegated foliage, set just inside the boundaries, can be used to produce contrast.

As with inanimate objects in the garden, the scale of plants must be carefully considered, and if small trees are planted, the shrubs elsewhere should conform in size. The herbaceous areas should be densely-packed with high-quality plants, to encourage and maximize year-round interest. Many of the larger members of the alpine group and the smaller border plants would be suitable

choices; and their flowers should be considered in relation to their foliage characteristics. In general, the inevitable competition for light in a small, densely planted garden means that it is wise to choose plants that will thrive in the shade.

Fruit and vegetables can be grown successfully, in small quantities, without adversely affecting the general appearance of a small garden. Raspberries and loganberries look well grown along walls, and attractive bushes, yielding crops such as gooseberries and high-bush blueberries, can combine with apple or plum trees as features of a shrubbery.

Lighting is sadly neglected in most gardens. Its effect can be romantic or, as in this case, otherworldly. Lighting next to paths and stairs has a key safety function.

In the same way, a few lettuces and a couple of bush tomato and strawberry plants among the general planting look appealing and yet, at the same time, satisfy the husbandy instincts.

EARTHWORKS

To establish a time-frame for the comprehensive replanning of a small garden, it is helpful to think in terms of a three-year plan. In it, the initial tasks would comprise major earthworks, drainage and soil treatment, followed by construction of walls, paths, pergolas and planting posts. By the first autumn, it could be possible to plant most of the trees and all the climbers at the foot of the walls. In the second year, most of the shrubs could be planted and any patio work completed. In an ideal world, by early in year three, most of the rest of the planting—a few additional shrubs—and all the perennial herbaceous plants and bulbs could be in place. From then on, the garden simply demands tidying and tinkering—moving plants to better locations and adding varieties to improve the effect.

In such a scheme, moving earth is not only the first but also one of the heaviest tasks, and it does pay to use a contractor to do this mechanically if possible. Modern earthmoving machines can maneuver themselves through gaps of only $3\frac{1}{2}$ft (1m) and are capable of moving and digging as much earth in one day as a strong man could move in several months with a wheelbarrow and shovel. They are invaluable for digging out unwanted tree stumps and obdurate roots. Machines are also efficient at raking aside topsoil from the working area, excavating subsoil to be used in building up and leveling other areas of the garden and then replacing the topsoil, leaving the entire area smooth and tidy.

The character of the soil itself is obviously of prime importance in planning any garden. It is virtually impossible to grow lime-hating plants on soils with a high alkaline or limestone content. Soils in mature gardens may have become acid over the years and will benefit by a good dressing of lime while preparing the land, prior to planting. Similarly, if the soil is excessively light or extremely heavy, it is worthwhile adding a good loam from elsewhere, before any planting begins. If only a small planting area is involved, the nature of the topsoil can be radically changed with imported loam. However, if the subsoil is a badly drained and sticky clay, it would pay to improve the drainage.

DRAINAGE

It is important to ensure adequate drainage in the initial planning stages because many plants will not tolerate or grow in saturated soil. One way to test existing drainage from the garden is to dig a hole at least 30in (76cm) deep after a long spell of rainy weather. This is then filled with water, and the rate at which the level drops is noted. If it takes more than 24 hours to drain away completely, putting in an artificial drainage system is an option that should be seriously considered. If the problem is slight, an earth-mover can be used simply to dig a deep sump at the lowest point in the garden. Filled with gravel and topped with soil, this will act as a "soakaway".

If the problem is more serious, the services of a landscape architect or other drainage expert will be needed. This sometimes complicated matter of correct drainage must be solved before the garden is planted. Problems arising later will be even harder to solve without virtually destroying the garden.

OPTIONS

Every situation in small garden planning can be met by a wide choice of options: it is a mistake to think that behind every garden that needs attention there is a single ideal garden lurking like a ghost that needs to be coaxed out of hiding and given flesh. There are actually many variables that will determine your approach.

First, there are the requirements of the site. Seaside gardens, for example, may need special treatment—perhaps some kind of screening feature to provide shelter against salt-laden wind, and a selection of robust plants tolerant of poor coastal soil. On the other hand, some seaside sites in temperate zones are washed by warm ocean currents, giving you the chance to grow sub-tropical plants that would not be feasible inland.

Another factor is the microclimate—the set of local conditions in a garden, including soil type, aspect and structure. Walls of stone or brick retain heat, and thus make a good backing for tender plants. The amount of sunlight received is determined partly by the slope of the land. Walls and trees cast longer midday shadows in winter, when the sun is not so high in the sky. Such considerations may seem peripheral, but they can be all-important when it comes to choosing the planting.

Then there is the question of personal needs. The garden has certain functions to perform, just like a room of the house, but these functions will vary from household to household. Will the garden be used for parties or just for gentle relaxation? Is a kitchen garden needed, with space for herbs and vegetables? Children are a crucial factor. In my own experience, there is little point in spending too much time and money on creating an exquisite small garden if young children are likely to use it as a play area. However, there are plenty of passionate gardeners who are also caring parents, so perhaps for some people this is the kind of

warning to be listened to and then forgotten.

Remember that the needs of the family evolve in time, and take this into account. If children are expected in the future, you can make a pool if you wish, but make sure that it can be easily filled in and turned into another kind of feature. An obvious precaution is to avoid anything with poisonous berries or seeds, such as yew or laburnum.

The elderly and infirm may need to be provided for. If so, steps should be easy to negotiate—not too steep and winding—and there should be something to hang on to for a steady balance. Raised beds, retained behind a wall, will take the bending and stretching out of routine maintenance.

Busy people as well as the aged or incapacitated will want to cut down on maintenance as much as possible. And of course there are plenty of people who find gardening a tiresome chore. Hard surfaces such as paving stones, brick and gravel need less tending than lawns. You can also save effort by avoiding labor-intensive plants that need a lot of pruning, staking and dead-heading. Most shrubs are easy to manage. Using ground cover planting to eliminate

(Continued on page 22)

A tiled mural provides a stylish—but expensive—solution to the common problem posed by the high wall of an adjacent building. Confronted with such a wall, you can distract attention from it, cover it with planting, or make an important feature of it. All these approaches can be successful if pursued vigorously. To prevent a conflict of interest in this example, the planting has been kept deliberately simple. Covering the whole wall area with tiles would have been excessive, so the design includes two contrasting foliage colors to mask the upper corners. The paving surface is gravel, edged with a surround of bricks. Compare this high-outlay, low-maintenance treatment with the alternative options overleaf.

A water system is another way to deal with the problem of a high wall. Here, water spilling over dams from a stepped arrangement of troughs finally arrives in a low-level canal which runs around two sides of the garden. A submerged pump concealed in a cistern below the canal not only recirculates the water but also powers a small plume fountain. One of the troughs has a "beard" of trailing plants instead of water—this is the kind of visual echo that always works well. Around the gravel surface, an L-shaped area of brickwork, edging a planted border, matches the shape of the canal—another visual echo. The gravel is softened by a small group of potted fuchsias, which also provide a link between the two levels. The flower colors in the garden have been deliberately restricted to reds and whites. Notice the overhanging bough from a neighboring garden: whatever our feelings about being overlooked, intrusions like this often work to our advantage.

Cladding the obtrusive wall with creepers such as ivy will not distract attention from it, but will create an agreeable backcloth for features placed prominently in the plot. Here, the gravel is restricted to an L-shaped sector which embraces a lawned area pierced by interesting planting, including a beautiful flowering cherry and a handsome mountain ash for all-season interest. Trees like these provide useful shade for a seating area. Empty seats always evoke a sense of anticipation or a stir of memories, and provided that their design is compatible with the rest of the garden—all too often it is not—you need not be in a hurry to bring them inside.

(Continued from page 19)
weeds, and growing informal hedges, rather than formal ones, which require more frequent trimming, are sensible strategies. If you are a rose-lover, you might prefer to plant old-fashioned shrub roses, again to limit pruning requirements.

Taste and style dictate the garden plan in more nebulous ways. Certain observations can be offered, but only at the risk of finding plenty of exceptions to undermine the point. To avoid too hard and distinct a division between the house and the garden, it helps to have a scattering of container plants which you can move around, or bring indoors, for a versatile range of choices. You can also grow climbers against the house, or use hanging baskets or window boxes.

Curves will be an improvement on straight lines in many situations, unless you want a deliberately formal effect. Certainly this applies to the edges of lawns, which are all too often blank, boring rectangles.

Color needs to be handled with care. Too many vivid colors jostling against each other are likely to make the viewer feel uneasy; most people prefer subtle harmonies or controlled contrasts of, for example, yellow and blue. To create a successful color composition, and one that provides interest throughout the year, it's essential to choose plants carefully. Make a chart of the proposed planting and fill in the flowering times to see where they coincide. Don't neglect to consider foliage, as this too can add a bright splash of color. A single-color garden (white is the most popular) will work well within a foliage framework in shades of green and gray.

Happily, there are very few rules governing garden design. Many of the guidelines given above can be broken with creative effect, provided that the transgressions are made with flair and confidence.

A good example of a rule that may be turned on its head would be the dictum that a long, narrow lot should be made to look wider by including features such as paths, screens, walls and so on set transversely across it. This is a ploy that has worked well in a million small gardens. However, many excellent gardens have also been made following the opposite approach – that is, creating an "alley garden", in which length and narrowness are turned into virtues. Such gardens can be given a distinctly Elizabethan feel by creating a series of buttress-like features in pairs down the sides of the plot – for example, hedges, or boxes of trellis work – leaving a central pathway of gravel or close-mown lawn. To lead the eye directly down the alley to the end of the plot, some obvious feature such as a piece of sculpture, a fountain or even a column-shaped or brightly colored tree or shrub can be stationed here. The tunnel effect could be further exaggerated by linking the short lateral projections with overhead arches of trellis, ironwork or foliage. Such a scheme produces an obvious "walk", which commands exploration. To give variety to the alley, the areas hidden from view behind the lateral projections might be treated in different ways. Beyond one pair of projections there could be paved areas with pedestals and busts; beyond another there might be herbs planted in a patterned ground-level bed with espaliered fruit trees on the walls.

Another strongly held belief is that there should always be a balance between several features – that a garden should contain a little of everything, including lawn, shrubbery, paving and herbaceous beds. However, many designers have discarded this notion with wonderful results. A garden based on a single prominent theme – like the azalea garden on pages 100–101 or the Japanese evergreen garden on pages 124–7 – can often have a stunning impact.

A cloistered atmosphere, reminiscent of the secluded court of an oriental temple, characterizes this paved garden surrounded by dense planting. The horizontal emphasis, with discreet changes of level, helps to create an overall tranquility. There is nothing frenzied about the planting to destroy the sense of calm. The rounded stones of the ground surface are not so regularly sized or placed that they become monotonous. Weathered railroad ties retain the raised beds and offer abundant seating–a use suggested by the relaxed classical pose of the Buddha statue used to provide a focal point. On the other corner a shallow ceramic vessel, with its thin film of water, demonstrates a way of introducing this vital element to a garden without the need for ambitious works. At the bottom of the garden, a thick hedge of varying foliage is backed by planting on a neigboring lot. Against such an evergreen profusion, it takes only a few small flowering plants in the raised beds to shine out in vivid contrast. Other ideas that play on the same themes are illustrated overleaf.

A livelier effect could be created with little modification in the garden illustrated on page 23, which might be too sober for some tastes. In this illustration, the darkness of surrounding vegetation has been used as foil for bright trellis work fencing. Such a web of white or other pale-colored woodwork could look pretty on its own, or be draped in flowering climbers. The central arch, also a prime spot for climbers, creates vertical interest to balance the weeping tree. It would look spectacular planted with a wisteria or climbing hydrangea. The seat is simple but effectively placed to make the most of scent from the planting on the trellis.

A more radical treatment would be to replace the paving with softer lawn, in addition to the changes shown opposite, and alter the character of the raised beds by introducing more color and foliage interest. The main bed could include a pond, from which a rock and gravel bank emerge, as shown in the illustration. Mound-forming plants in this area might include golden or green thyme, with small trees such as *Juniperus communis* providing vertical accents.

Above **In other areas** of the garden, traditional cottage garden plants such as lupines, foxgloves, lavender and roses might be included to create a show of informal color. You should try to combine different flower shapes, with tall spikes at the back, as shown above.

25

Above **The L-shaped garden** shown here has been designed for easy maintenance. Staggering the paving stones has prevented a long corridor-like effect, and the planting along the borders is designed to be labor-saving. The timber fence and the paving itself are stepped to create an interesting, although shallow change of level. A changing color palette in a garden like this could easily be achieved by judicious use of bulbs such as tulips. (This garden is described in more detail on pages 92–3.)

A composition such as this—a kind of still life of plants, stones and ornament—could easily be introduced into the garden on the opposite page. The plants have been thoughtfully chosen to present maximum variety of color, form and texture. Large-leaved *Rheum palmatum* contrasts with sword-like *Phormium tenax* and a delicate clump of ornamental grass. Ivy on the fence provides a backdrop. Around the pot are gray-leaved *Helichrysum* and *Senecio maritimus*, sharply offset by poppies. *Sedum* creates an attractive texture at ground level.

A pergola frame and stag's horn sumac tree offer an interesting alternative to the design shown in the photograph opposite, turning the seating area into a shady retreat paved with old mellow bricks under a parasol of foliage. The pergola could be roofed and walled with glass panels, but in this case provision would have to be made for a waterproof surround to the tree trunk. This is the type of arrangement frequently adopted with success by owners of garden restaurants. The "corridor" of the garden has also been transformed to make it much more informal, with stepping stones rising from gravel and ground-covering baby's tears (*Helxine solierolii*) like rocks from a sea. The interest of New Zealand flax (*Phormium tenax*), blue-flowering *Ajuga reptans* and other plants at the pergola entrance is reinforced by a large pot—such pots can look attractive even when left unplanted.

27

A JAPANESE GARDEN

A provoking serenity characterizes most Japanese gardens. This makes the Japanese style ideal for people with a busy life who need a calm atmosphere to relax in from time to time. Because of their sparseness, such gardens require very little maintenance. However, because they are so delicate and subtle, some owners might find them incompatible with young children.

The aura of changelessness intrinsic to the true Japanese garden is achieved by planting a high proportion of evergreens. With a few notable exceptions such as azaleas and magnolias, evergreens do not have showy flowers. The feeling of serenity is reinforced by the wonderfully clean lines of the artifacts traditionally used to complete the effect: these are mostly made of bamboo or stone.

What makes Japanese gardens so interesting—and ultimately so satisfying—is their inherent symbolism. Each plot contains a world of visual metaphors, stemming from the tradition of nature worship which lies at the heart of the Shinto religion. For example, a boulder in the garden might be revered as a symbol of a god, its position determined with the care of a priest arranging a sacrament on an altar. Or the same boulder might be used to denote a huge mountain dominated by a plain—represented by the garden's ground surface.

1 Bamboo fence against wall of house

2 Water basin with bamboo channel (see page 31)

3 Bamboo railing marks edges of paving

4 Stone Japanese-style ornament (see page 30)

5 Mature tree

6 Bamboo stool

7 Wall clad in ivy

8 Gravel surface

9 Rockery with clump of bamboo

10 Brick paving with uneven edge

11 Meandering paving stones

12 Stone Buddha

Above **Brick paving** (10), left over from the original garden before it was redesigned, has been preserved as a hard surface that contrasts well with gravel. This would be a novel treatment for a paved barbecue or seating area, instead of the usual straight edge.
● Old brickwork can often be re-used in new ways when a garden is redesigned.

Left **Picturesque clumps** of bamboo and paths of stepping stones through a gravel bed are typically Japanese features. The meandering routes provide a series of views of the garden from different angles, making the plot appear deceptively larger. The stones are set into the gravel at different depths to give each one a different emphasis.
● Flat gravel represents placid water. The Japanese also rake sand or fine gravel into furrows to represent a choppy sea. This can be imitated in a small garden, but keeping the gravel neatly raked is time-consuming and requires some skill.

A clean contrast between rock, gravel, grasses and ground cover represents the best in Japanese-style gardening. This detail is taken from the rockery in one corner.

Near right **Grasses**, ferns, spotted laurel and a Japanese maple (*Acer palmatum*) form a natural parasol of leaves over a water basin, making a secluded feature (2).
● Miniature landscapes such as this are excellent features for a garden corner.

Far right **A water conduit**, leading to the basin surrounded by pebbles, has been fashioned from a pierced length of bamboo. Two lengths of bamboo resting crossways on the basin's lip help to give visual strength to the feature, preventing the spout from seeming too isolated.
● To draw attention to a small water feature such as this, it is a good idea to allow a jet to spray over boulders, which are thus permanently wet. However, this entails some water loss, so the sump from which the water is recirculated must have a replenishing supply.

Right **A stone Buddha** (12) peeps through a screen of foliage, which casts camouflaging shadows. The frame of bamboo behind is an inexpensive but effective way to add an oriental feel to a plain white wall.

Tight bamboo fencing against the house wall (1) announces the Japanese style of the garden and provides an interesting textured background. The bamboo theme is reiterated in the bamboo stool on the brick terrace and the little bamboo fence.

● Japanese stone lanterns, like the one shown here, are available from many garden ornament manufacturers. Some have tops carved with ridges to support moss or bird food.

PAVING AROUND MATURITY

A mature tree is an asset in any garden—even if it is right in the middle of the lot. Here, the designer has exploited the central tree to break the uniformity of a low-maintenance garden dominated by stone paving slabs. There is nothing bleak about this design. The paving is successful partly because high-quality stone has been used; and it has been made more interesting by being laid in rectangles of varying sizes. This simple treatment of the ground makes the garden seem much larger than it really is. To avoid any feeling of monotony, there is a small, lower terrace near the house.

Paving a garden containing a large tree is in fact usually far more satisfactory than trying to maintain a lawn. It is difficult to establish lush grass in the shady conditions created by the tree. Also, extensive tree roots tend to rob turf of the vital water which grass needs if it is to remain green and thriving.

Although a paved area requires little maintenance, bear in mind that in the fall a mature deciduous tree will shed thousands of leaves which will need sweeping up.

The shallow step to the large upper terrace in this garden is attractively curved to echo the curves of the classically beautiful double flight of iron-railed steps, leading from the house door into the garden.

2 False acacia

3 Pots containing yuccas, tobacco plants, trailing lobelia and ivy either side of two-seater chair

8 Elegant double flight of steps

1 Mature tree

4 Tables and chairs

5 Weathered stone paving

6 Low-level bedding

7 Shallow step

Above **A curved flight** of steps (8) is inevitably a notable feature in the design of a small garden such as this. The steps fan down on to delicately planted raised beds, containing senecio, lacecap hydrangeas, bamboos and *Cotoneaster horizontalis*.

Above **The striped foliage** and soft texture of the virulent ground cover plant, *Lamium maculatum*, makes a delightful contrast with the hard stone paving. A transitional area is provided by scattering bold, sea-smoothed pebbles among the plants.

Above right **The yuccas** dotted around the garden create a tropical ambience.
● Yuccas include some of the hardiest exotic-looking plants, such as *Y. filamentosa*. The more tender species may be grown in containers for summer display, overwintering under glass.

Right **Tight planting** in a pot (3) demonstrates how just a small quantity of compost can be made to support plenty of flowers and foliage when land is at a premium. The delicate blue-green leaves of rue are entwined with the sharp, spindly yucca, which dominates. At

their base are profusely flowering tobacco plants, feverfew and lobelia, with variegated ivy spilling over the edge of the decorative terracotta pot.

RUSTIC REDS

Here is a fine demonstration of the fact that a garden paved with highly durable materials need not feel harsh. The uncompromising smoothness of the paving is modulated by the broken surface of the gravel, to produce a pleasing background for carefully chosen plants. The smooth, new look of the brick paving is part of its appeal: a more traditional approach would have been to use old worn bricks, creating an effect of mellow rusticity rather than graphic precision.

The choice of the purple-leaved smoke tree (*Cotinus Coggygria* 'Purpureus') to dominate the terrace is unusual and audacious. Its foliage—purple turning light red in the fall—contrasts beautifully with the light gravel· beyond. The tree also provides a fine, dark curtain against which the tall, elegant blue-flowered *Agapanthus* and yellow day lilies are displayed.

The dignity and stature of these plants is emphasized by the charm of the miniature alpine plants, such as the little mound-forming saxifrages, which have been thoughtfully raised closer to eye level by planting them in a water barrel.

1 Lawn

2 Shrubbery

3 Gravel

4 Lean-to conservatory

5 Potted zonal pelargoniums in sunken area

6 *Sedum spectabile* in large pot

7 Barbecue on base

8 Water barrel containing alpines

9 Large bread crock used as ornament

10 Paved terrace in clean new bricks

11 Smoke bush (*Cotinus Coggygria* 'Purpureus')

Left **A mass of flower color**, including the vivid red of impatience, is thrown into prominence by the dark smoke tree (11). In the far corner of the garden, a sumac (*Rhus typhina*) spreads its canopy: in the fall this will turn brilliant red or orange, echoing the smoke tree.

Above **The lean-to conservatory** (4), echoing the pitch of the house roof, provides a fine transition between the house and the garden proper, especially when filled with plants. Note how the contrast between the brick terracing and the gravel has been emphasized by a slightly raised surface. A tub of *Sedum spectabile* (6) marks the corner of the terrace.
● A large conservatory (4) reduces the amount of space for planting outdoors, but the benefits are quite apparent in winter.
● A barbecue (7) can be a permanent garden feature. Here it is small and unobtrusive, with a base of loose bricks and paving slabs.

PLANTING BETWEEN PAVING

High-quality paving and walling used as a background for a superb variety of plants make an unbeatable basis for a garden. When the quality of planting and materials is as impressive as in this small town plot, there is no need for an intricate layout or for eyecatching ornaments. The plants themselves, surrounding and interspersed among the paving stones, wonderfully varied in shape, texture and color, provide all the ornament necessary. They range from the tall, dark, column-like shape of the Irish yew (*Taxus baccata* 'Fastigiata') to the wispy, silvery foliage of the *Artemisia arborescens* which stands next to the house door.

A large proportion of the planting is evergreen, with foliage in subtle hues of yellow, green and grey. Succulents give parts of the garden a distinctive Mediterranean feel. To prevent any garishness, flower color is largely restricted to yellow, white and pink. Herbs such as rosemary and sage would marry well with the overall style.

The central area of the garden is a raised stone platform with a paved top where plants grow in little pockets of soil. Built on one corner of the platform is a small raised bed of gray-leaved *Senecio compactus*. The boundary is an unobtrusive open-weave fence, which apart from a few gaps is covered with foliage.

Around the door a wealth of foliage arrests the eye. To the right, fronds of *Artemisia arborescens* (2) contrast with arching *Acanthus spinosus*, whose flower stalks retain a few white petals. To the left are the yellow seedheads of *Clematis viticella* and another *Artemisia*.

● Gray-leaved plants, usually resistant to drought and heat, are not always hardy enough for northern gardens.

1 Raised beds

2 *Artemisia arborescens*

3 Paving stones

4 Trellis with clematis

5 Platform capped with stone

6 Raised bed of *Senecio compactus*

A view across the central platform to the boundary presents a rich pattern of leaf forms. Around the edge are *Sedum spectabile*, the flopping, woolly leaves of *Stachys lanata* and *Bergenia cordifolia*, with its large, leathery green leaves. On the platform, the greys of more *Stachys lanata*, *Senecio compactus* (6) and the gently arching *Helichrysum petiolatum* provide a striking counterfoil to the metallic reddish-purple *Ajuga reptans* 'Purpurea', which bears small blue flowers in summer.
● Bergenias are useful ground cover plants. Their evergreen leaves often take on a red tinge in the fall.

At one corner of the platform, a columnar Irish yew (*Taxus baccata* 'Fastigiata') contrasts with a mound of saxifrage at its foot.

WALLS WITHIN WALLS

A garden planned with hard, crisp lines can be extremely satisfying. Rather than attempting to disguise the fact that the garden is tightly constricted within brick walls, the designer has made a virtue of the situation and introduced brick paving and more brick walls, with bold curves, to create a pervasive feeling of warmth and harmony. A simple and appealing brick archway has been built to surround the exit gate.

Interest has been heightened by two approximately L-shaped raised beds, creating an extra level. The space has become a cosy, sheltered outdoor room, surrounded by thoughtful planting. Running around one of the raised beds at its foot, note the little trough—a miniature, ground-level bed containing a selection of mound-forming plants such as *Calluna vulgaris*.

Although the plan is relatively basic, the shapes in this garden have been carefully arranged to maintain interest. A good bricklayer could transform a space of this size into a walled garden within a few days. However, it is important to bear in mind that the second-hand, well-weathered bricks which are intrinsic to the overall effect could represent a costly initial outlay.

1 Brick walls topped by trellis panels

2 Brick arch over iron gate

3 Raised beds retained by brick walls

4 Brick trough at ground level

5 Pelargoniums in pots

6 Steps down into the garden

White cast-iron decorative furniture counteracts the somberness of so much plain brick. Massed pelargoniums dominate the planting theme in the promontory bed that projects from the wall to the base of the steps (6), their pink blooms making a good foil for the warm tones of the brickwork. When the pelargoniums are taken indoors to protect them from winter frost, some substitute may be desirable–for example, winter-flowering pansies.

● Raised beds (3), which you can work without having to bend, are an excellent labor-saving device. Those displayed here are a model of their type, with plenty of room for compost to support even the deepest-rooted plants.

THE ART OF TREILLAGE

In the great 17th-century French gardens of Versailles and elsewhere, a striking feature was the use of *treillage*–highly decorative trelliswork in complex architectural forms, often with latticed arches and columns. The garden illustrated here, a masterpiece of carpentry, deliberately evokes this tradition of the past. The patterning of the trellises is dense enough to give an impression of massive masonry. These structures are freestanding boundaries. However, arches of a similar kind –perhaps simplified to suit a lower budget– could equally well be placed against solid walls in a small town garden, and would have the effect of seeming to push out the boundaries.

Delicate trellises like this make an obvious showcase for climbing plants, but these must be chosen with care. Large-leaved climbers might be inappropriately heavy-looking: on tightly woven trellises it would be far better to choose a light, airy clematis.

Set into the main trellis panel here is a large mirror, crisscrossed by a lattice. This blocks out the neighboring garden, but will obviously reflect anyone using the bench. If the next-door plot is attractive, you might prefer an open diagonal lattice without the mirror– but more tightly spaced than this one for greater seclusion.

A low brick retaining wall within the trelliswork boundaries marks out a square with three shallow bays, one of which embraces a fine curved stone bench.

The diagonals of this herringbone brickwork paving echo the form of crisscrossed trelliswork behind the bench. The planting includes a sprinkling of annuals such as pink *Nicotiana* (2). This view, like the one opposite, shows the garden before the planting is properly established, but the overall design is strong enough to overcome a temporary sparseness of foliage and flower color.

1 Mirror flanked by shrubs

2 *Nicotiana alata* and other annuals

3 White stone bench

4 Raised beds with low brick walls match paving material: shrubs include viburnum, camellia, honeysuckle and abutilon

5 Complex architectural trelliswork

6 Steps leading into garden

7 Paving of bricks in herringbone pattern

The bench (3), raised on five scrolled bases, has an Italian Renaissance feel. The planting nearby includes, on the left of the mirrored trellis arch, a graceful tamarisk and a eucalyptus, supported by a stake. On the right is a 'Canary Bird' abutilon.

● Abutilons are evergreen shrubs with large maple-like leaves and pendulous bell-shaped flowers (early summer) in shades of red, orange, yellow, mauve or pink. They are not winter-hardy but will survive in a cool greenhouse.

●This eucalyptus (for warm, dry climates only) will remain evergreen and produce its small, blue leaves all year round if kept pruned to about 4ft.

A SQUARE WITHIN A SQUARE

This is a charming and intensely practical, low-maintenance design. The symmetry, and the uniformity of the paving, have been happily modified by raised beds and by a pond in one corner, with curved margins.

Further relief has been provided by treating the central ground area as a kind of masonry rug, with bricks and cobbles inset among the larger paving slabs. Much of the impact of the garden comes from this imaginative mixing of materials. One way to create further interest would be to omit paving slabs from the grid pattern to allow extra planting space.

A fast-growing *Ailanthus altissima* tree, planted through the paving, casts a deep shadow. A sumac (*Rhus typhina*) adds broken shade. Other parts of the garden receive full sunlight. There is thus a considerable variety of light and shade in a small area, opening up options for a broad range of plants with different growing requirements.

In a garden where many of the tones are subdued and restful, the selection of well-designed, white, cast-iron furniture provides a pleasing contrast, while marrying well with the cast-iron steps leading down into the garden.

The white tree seat around the trunk of the *Ailanthus*, apart from offering added shady seating in hot weather, gives the tree an attractive skirt and makes another bright feature to divert the eye.

1 *Ailanthus altissima* provides shelter

2 Shady seat around trunk

3 Raised pool

4 Screening plants on trellis

5 Central paving pattern of brick, cobbles and paving slabs

6 Hydrangeas in pots at entrance

Left **Bold hydrangeas** (6) look wonderful when allowed to break the monotony of a plain wall.
● Hydrangeas, or hortensias as they used to be known, look good in pots and make useful plants to combine with and enliven architectural features. If given enough moisture, they will do well at the foot of a shady wall. Pink or red hydrangeas turn blue if the soil is acid.

Above **Variegated ivy**, some fronds of *Helichrysum petiolatum* and the fat foliage of a *Sedum* soften the sharp edges of the wall of a raised bed. Bright-flowered, fragant tobacco plants stand out well against the shade cast by the *Ailanthus* foliage, in which hostas luxuriate. This kind of thoughtful, mixed planting combines both variety and practicality.

Left **The tiny pool** (3) reflecting surrounding foliage, enriches the whole garden experience. The stone pool margins are relieved by a spill of ivy (*Hedera colchica*) and purple-flowered *Campanula carpatica*.
● Small statues used in isolation can sometimes look somewhat lost. It may be preferable to choose a matching pair, as with these oriental demons. For the observant, a smaller statue lurks in the foliage behind.

43

A UNIVERSAL GARDEN

Here the landscaper has used a geometry set to create the ultimate low-maintenance garden. Circles of three sizes, two of brick and one of brick-bound water, have been satisfyingly arranged on a clean and well-proportioned rectangular plot. This kind of scheme is a classic: it can be successfully adapted to any climatic conditions anywhere in the world. For example, in a hot climate the design might look stunning with a generous grouping of monumental cacti.

Low brick walls raised on parts of the circles' circumferences hold back raised beds. About one-third of the total area is thickly planted. Most of the rest of the garden is paved with large rectangular slabs. The monotony of the hard surfaces has been successfully broken by selecting two totally different paving materials, by the slight raising of the brick circles, and by the contrast of circles and squares. The bricklaying required for the circles is perhaps more complicated than the simple pattern would suggest: each of the bricks inside the outer rim has to be carefully cut to shape.

A notable low-maintenance feature is the heavy preponderance of weed-stifling evergreens. Hebes, prostrate junipers, laurels, *Choisya ternata* and ivies feature strongly in the choice of planting, the *Choisya* (Mexican orange) providing white starry flowers in early summer. The evergreens are backed by deciduous plants such as *Clematis montana* and buddleia, for relief. In cold climates, hardier shrubs could substitute for hebe, laurel and *Choisya*.

Challengingly modern, this type of garden makes up in its geometric elegance for the lack of bold color in the planting. Many of the plants used are shade-loving, and flower color is limited—although there is a wealth of textures and tones in the foliage.

1 Lightweight timber fence supporting creepers

2 Circular pool, framed by brick

3 *Senecio*

4 Circles of patterned brick

5 Hebes break circle

6 Mat-forming ground cover

7 Paved terrace

8 Path to raised terrace

Left **The pure geometry** of this garden harmonizes with the uncluttered lines of a modern house. However, in summer it will be difficult to resist the temptation to place some attractive urns on the brick terraces and plant them with annuals for a splash of color.

● Circles in garden plans can be made more interesting by allowing an intrusion, such as the arc of another circle or a promontory of planted bed, to break the perfection of their circumference. We often feel uncomfortable when faced with perfect symmetry. A little imperfection can be reassuring, and if the line of a circle is broken (as it is by the hebes in this example: 5) the eye will subconsciously etch in the missing track.

● Fences of this kind, with wide gaps between thin vertical timbers, create excellent visual screens while not appearing too heavy and imposing. Unlike solid fences, they are unlikely to blow down in a high wind.

Right **Moving water** can easily be introduced into a garden: you do not need an elaborate fountain or carved spout. Provided that the source is disguised, as here (2), a simple hose is adequate. The pool is surprisingly small—one of several ways in which the garden departs from orthodox planning.

45

SHADES OF DECEPTION

The planting in this small romantic town garden has been so ingeniously contrived that when viewed from the window it is impossible to judge the extent of the plot beyond the point where the brick paving peters out.

This deception has been achieved by arranging plants to flow out from both margins toward the center of the garden, and at this point allowing only a narrow passageway between. A natural archway, created beneath a dome of tight topiary on the left and the splendidly contrasting spikiness of the palm-like cordyline on the right, further isolates the area beyond. (The cordyline is hardy only in southern Florida and Hawaii; a good substitute elsewhere might be a spiky conifer or unpruned *Magnolia stellata*.) Among the tangle of hostas, ferns, lacecap hydrangea and other plants of strong character, a small square pool has been carefully sited where it can be appreciated from the house. The forms in the middle ground are so strong that they distract attention from the side walls, which are further subdued by a layer of dark ivy.

Once the foliage curtain has been penetrated, the garden opens out again and the surface changes from brick to lawn. From the secluded seat the house is no longer visible. Adjacent to this seating area, a large-flowered clematis offers itself for contemplation.

This garden is an excellent example of how to use changes in light intensity effectively. The dark foreground "compartment" precedes a bright, open area with a somber background beyond (see also pages 48–9).

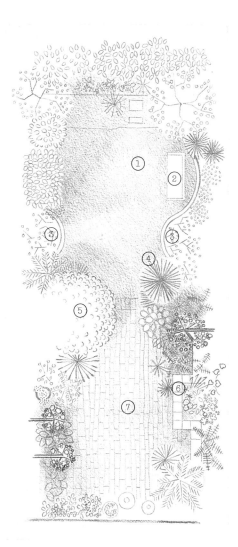

1 Lawn

2 Stone seat

3 Low raised beds retained by flint wall

4 Cordyline

5 Trimmed laurel (*Prunus laurocerasus*)

6 Small pool with lion waterspout, draped with two types of ivy (page 48)

7 Brickwork in approximate rectangular pattern

Bold planting, with distinct forms and leaf shapes, is particularly satisfying when included in the view from the house.
● Topiary, the practice of cutting trees and bushes into ornamental shapes, is becoming fashionable again. The two most popular materials, for large and small shapes respectively, are yew and box, but in this case laurel (*Prunus laurocerasus*) (5) has been used instead. Except in rigidly formal designs, too much topiary can make a garden feel unnatural. Here, however, it is sensitively used to create a contrast with the undisciplined tousle of the cabbage palm (*Cordyline australis*) (4) at the foot of which is a clump of large-leaved *Hosta fortunei*.

Left **Old mellow bricks** around the square pool (6) have been laid with a deliberate trace of crookedness to avoid too regular an impression.
● Brick paving may convey or reinforce a variety of different moods, depending on the patterns it makes. Here, an arrangement of concentric rectangles gives an impression of stillness, forcing the visitor to slow his pace. A path of bricks laid lengthways or zigzagging along in a herringbone would have the opposite effect of encouraging speed.

Above **A lion's head** set over the pool emits a trickle of water and conjures up classical associations. Embedded stones add subtle interest to the pool's surround.
● It is often effective, in architectural features of this kind, to contrast two different types of ivy, one large-leaved and one with smaller, variegated leaves, as here.

Above **A couchant hound** draws the eye in the area of the garden most remote from the house. Around the lawn, stones have been used to retain the curved raised beds. Also incorporated into the pool surround shown on the opposite page, the stones create a sense of continuity between the two distinct areas of the garden. Lacecap hydrangeas in the foreground harmonize well with *Clematis Jackmanii* 'Superba' cladding the right-hand boundary.

A FOREST CLEARING

This lovely small town garden contains many of the classic features that keen gardeners love— mixed shrubbery, lawn, lots of beautiful shrub roses and generous open and shady areas permitting an interesting mix of herbaceous planting. The great strength of the design is the way in which the various elements have been combined to achieve pleasing harmony.

A terrace for dry seating near the house, made from simple rectangular paving slabs, is spacious and distinctive without being overwhelming.

The two shallow steps leading up from the terrace to the lawn denote a subtle change in level. Their impact is deliberately subdued: in this garden it is the plants, rather than hard architecture, that command most attention. Although a relatively large area of the garden is devoted to lawn, this is framed by an informal edge of massed foliage, which makes it seem like a forest glade, stumbled upon by accident.

1 Well-trimmed lawn

2 Paved terrace

3 Trelliswork

4 Urn containing a plume of grasses marks change in level

5 Potted pelargoniums for splash of red in summer

6 Ferns and other shade-loving plants thrive under mature trees

7 Elegant garden furniture

8 Lavender

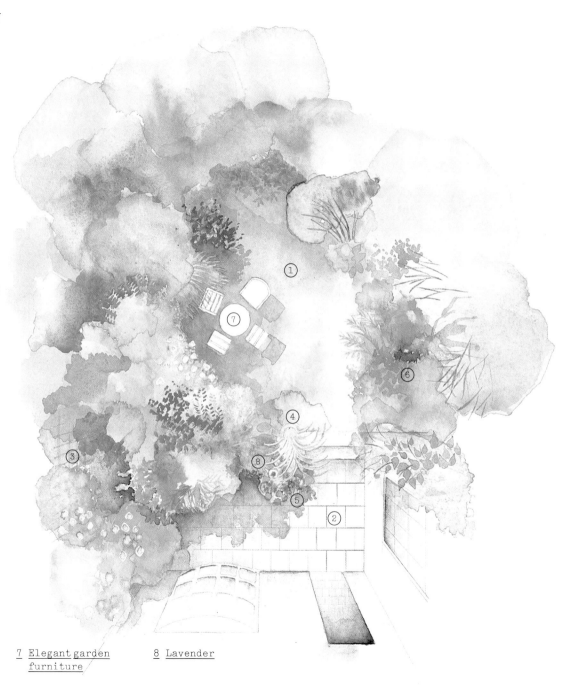

Left **A collar of ivy** surrounds the trunk of an old crab apple tree. The leafy canopy provides shady conditions ideal for ferns. The planting around this lawn is so dense and natural-looking that it gives the impression of being deep in the countryside.

Above **This slender grass**, a *Miscanthus* reminiscent of a water jet, makes a charming foreground eyecatcher. On the steps directly below are pelargoniums in pots which can be taken indoors out of the frost. Their luscious flowers always make a pleasing contrast with masonry. Beautiful urns and vases are best left unplanted, but here the rule has been broken to fine effect. To the left of the pots is a drift of lavender.

●Lavender (*Lavendula angustifolia*) has aromatic flowers and leaves. Even in mid-winter the foliage gives out its distinctive scent. The flowers appear between mid-summer and early fall, and range in color from deep purple to white. Lavender is excellent as an edging plant or low hedge.

51

CONTROLLED PLANTING

In this typically-proportioned town garden, overlooked by neighbors on all sides, the main design ploy is to assail the visitor with the charm of profuse vegetation. New delights are discovered at every step, distracting attention from the urban surroundings. To apply this seemingly simple approach requires year-round devotion to gardening and thorough planning, so that there is a wealth of interest in different seasons.

A strength of this garden is its sensitive use of color, which is plentiful without being garish. Reds, apart from the fuchsia, have largely been avoided. (Some people find this a good rule in a small garden, as the contrast between red and green can be too strong, holding the eye to the detriment of other plants nearby.) Good use has been made of different-colored foliage, acting as a foil for the changing colors of the flowers. The lawn has been left large enough for relaxation or play, but without taking precedence over the rest of the garden.

The overall effect is not of an unkempt jungle, nor of an abandoned garden returning to nature. Rather, this is a controlled planting scheme, with a definite form and intriguing color combinations.

The seating area near the house, shaded by a flowering cherry tree, is simple and uncluttered. Here, as in the rest of the garden, the temptation to "overdesign" with too much masonry, furniture and ornament has been resisted. The borders are designed to provide a glorious profusion in summer, notably with sweetpeas, lilies, ladies-mantle (*Alchemilla mollis*) and roses.

1 *Clematis* on house wall

2 Sheltered wooden bench

3 *Hydrangea villosa*

4 Herbaceous borders containing *Alchemilla mollis* and *Acanthus spinosus*

5 Stone paving

6 Lawn area

7 Climbing roses

8 Fuchsia in movable pot next to garden shed

The white door of the garden shed draws our gaze between densely planted borders to the end of the lawn. Languid white hosta flowers (right) are overhung by lax fronds of the hardy *Fuchsia magellanica* (8), behind which stands a tall hydrangea. Iris scimitars and, in the foreground, *Alchemilla mollis* and blue-green rue (*Ruta graveolens*) add to the effect of luxuriance. The opposite border (left) features more iris clumps, *Acanthus spinosus*, a dogwood (*Cornus alba* 'Elegantissima') and lining the path, white-flowered *Nicotiana alata* and *Sedum spectabile*. This photograph was taken in mid-summer: the azalea (foreground) would have provided a solid mound of color earlier in the season.

A SLATE GARDEN

This garden has been carefully planned to do justice to a house of great character, built in slate—the local stone. The materials chosen for the structure of the garden harmonize perfectly with the dwelling itself. The emphasis is on natural, muted colors, especially browns and grays, avoiding plastic troughs and planters or any other items that would introduce an undesirable synthetic element.

In the paving, the mixture of various textures, shapes and scales creates an interesting, irregular pathway. So abundant and packed is the mixed planting scheme that the exact route of the path is difficult to detect—making the garden all the more intriguing. A unifying theme is provided by the paved concrete circles, specially made in a disc-shaped mold. Unusual ornaments create a highly individual yet stylish effect.

Such a highly detailed and ornamental garden can be made for surprisingly little outlay. Often, the most appealing garden accessories are obtained by re-using items such as unwanted park benches, railroad ties or old slabs of marble, rather than commissioned pieces which may look out of style.

1 Secluded area

2 Raised pathway

3 Renovated bench painted green

4 Raised stone troughs containing rock plants

5 Concrete discs surrounded by pebbles set in mortar

6 Semi-circular raised bed surrounding permanent stone seat

7 Steps leading up from basement

8 Steps leading down from house

A busy, cottagey feel has been created around the house by using a variety of small rockery plants in stone troughs (4) and in the raised bed (6) with its curving stone wall. Note the harmonizing group of pink flowers in the foreground—thrift (*Armeria maritima*), pinks (*Dianthus*) and the tall columbine (*Aquilegia vulgaris*).

Right **Well-worn bricks** make a fine base for the sitting area with its white bench, setting it apart from the main path. The raised semi-circular beds create an attractive surround for the seat (which is backed by *Hebe pinguifolia* 'Pagei') and make optimum use of the contours of the lot. The laburnum tree (*L. anagyroides*) and the viburnum supported by a green cane create prominent vertical accents.

Above, top **Bamboo pea canes** are bound together to form a diagonal-patterned trellis. Backed by a white-painted wall, they provide an unusual support for a climbing rose and a wisteria and a good background for pot-grown dwarf conifers and a hart's-tongue fern.

Above **The charred remains** of an old log makes an excellent niche for *Sedum*, saxifrage and a dwarf juniper, embraced by a mound of the succulent *Cotyledon oppositifolium*.
● A log such as this will accommodate plants if drilled and the hole filled with peat.

AROUND AN APPLE TREE

The dominating apple tree creates a calm, romantic focal point in the heart of this garden. Other notable features are the ingenuity of planting and the richness of detail. A multitude of experiences has been packed into a small area. This is a good example of how different styles can be mingled successfully. The herbaceous borders sound a traditional country-cottage note, while toward the back of the garden a distinct Japanese influence can be seen in the meandering stepping-stones and the pond bounded by pebbles.

The high quality of the stone perimeter path sets the tone for the whole garden. This path is a decorative feature as much as a functional one, its appeal stemming from its purposeful simplicity. Paving stones such as these are available in standard sizes from garden centers. Their advantage, apart from their inherent beauty, is that they are small enough for paving intricate shapes. To make them comfortable to walk on, stones like these need to be laid on a deep bed of mortar.

The trellis work that forms the boundary of the garden has been reinforced, to mask neighboring buildings, by thin planks that obliterate some of the holes. This unusual fence offers a fine support for climbing roses and deciduous shrubs such as the fragrant *Philadelphus* 'Belle Etoile' to lean on.

An octagonal bench will add character to a spindly tree such as the apple tree (6) that dominates this lawn.
● As an alternative to the apple tree, you could obtain a similarly romantic effect with other trees from the Rose family. Examples include: *Prunus mume*, a delicate Japanese species which bears scented pale pink or white flowers on spindly green branches in mid-winter; and *Prunus yedoensis*, with slightly coarser, scented branches and pinkish white flowers in spring.

● When buying a tree, you should carefully consider the height to which it is likely to grow in 10 years time.

1 Secluded seat

2 Pond surrounded by ferns and stones

3 Japanese-style area with meandering paving stones

4 Path of stones edging herbaceous border

5 Climbing roses on trellis

6 Mature apple tree with octagonal bench

7 Brick walls topped by trellis work

8 Small flight of steps up to lawn

Above **Beach pebbles** make a splendid shore to a natural-looking pond (2). The duckweed in the pond has been allowed to prosper in the shade. The old log makes a fine division between the pond proper and a marshy area in which a hart's tongue and male fern (*Dryopteris Filix-mas*) luxuriate. The white shrubby chrysan-themum provides abundant flowers for much of the year.

Above right **Climbing roses** trained on the trellis, above a generously planted mixture including foxgloves, hostas, *Hydrangea arborescens*, pink petunias and a yellow-flowering *Potentilla* create a luxurious herbaceous border. The annuals—including petunias—provide extra splashes of color. In the foreground is a herb pot containing *Campanula isophylla*, and ivy.

Right **A candytuft's** white summer flowers stand out against a mound of *Nertera*. To the left is *Geranium sanguineum*—a complementary (but somewhat invasive) ground cover plant, as it produces deep pink flowers from early summer onwards.
● The candytuft (*Iberis sempervirens*) rapidly forms mats over dry walls. Tolerant of smoke and grime, it is well suited to towns.

THE BEAUTY OF HYDRANGEAS

In a small garden, a single highly-decorative iron seat situated at its extremity can become a potent attraction which lures the eye down the garden. Here an iron seat has been used in just this way to pull the sight line down to lawn level and distract attention from buildings beyond the end wall.

The overhanging canopy of a tree and the dense, tall planting close to the terrace mask views beyond the garden very effectively, making the sitting area a large, leafy arbor, with an intense feeling of privacy.

In such sheltered conditions, a single hydrangea, if well fed and watered, can provide a massive plant feature. Its bold foliage will dominate the foreground for a long season and a battery of cheerful flowers will provide color until late in the fall. Even when the color fades, the attractive heads in pastel shades will command attention long into the winter.

Although in this design the terrace is well shaded, provision has been made for sun worshippers on the upstairs balcony.

1 Hydrangeas

2 White-painted seat serves as eyecatcher

3 Steps flanked by curved raised beds

4 Mixed planting including *Hypericum calycinum*

5 Semi-circular raised bed beneath window

Left **A distinctive awning** and a screen of vegetation make this terrace into a kind of outdoor room. The yellow flowers are St John's wort (*Hypericum calycinum*).

Far left **The two hydrangeas** (1) that project toward the center of the lawn conceal the size of this garden–deliberately, you cannot see what lies beyond them. There could well be an extensive piece of garden to the left of the seat, but in fact there is just a small utility area.
● The lawn in a small garden should, ideally, be kept as beautifully shaved as it is here. Any attempt to convert a small patch of grass into a flower meadow tends to create untidiness.

Left **The bright evergreen** *Griselinia* (upper right) contrasts well with darker vegetation all around. A *Clematis montana* and an ivy take advantage of the support offered by the simple wooden staircase. Iris leaves stand out distinctly in the foreground. Overhanging the wall are rue (*Ruta graveoleus*) and *Ballota pseudodictamnus*.

59

WILDERNESS BETWEEN HOUSE AND STREET

Front gardens tend to be treated rather sparsely—perhaps a patch of lawn with flower beds or trees—but there is no reason why you shouldn't adopt a more adventurous style. Unusually, this front plot takes an informal approach, creating the feel of a wild cottage garden. To reach the house from the street, we pick our way along a narrow, angled path through a glorious jungle of plants—including phormium, helichrysums, santolina, day lilies, aloes and hydrangea. (In northern climates, you could choose from a wide range of substitutes for the more tender plants in this list.) The path alternates between moss-softened stone slabs and weathered brickwork whose crevices are filled with intricate mound-forming plants.

A dense front garden such as this not only creates seclusion around the house but also has a sound-proofing effect, insulating the residents from traffic noise. Moreover, wildlife is likely to be attracted, adding to the impression of a rural retreat.

The cultivated untidiness of the garden—with untrimmed shrubs, fallen leaves and moss growing in the paths—looks totally unplanned, and indeed that is the essence of its appeal. However, to create a garden like this from scratch you need to plan over a long timescale and consider carefully such factors as circulation routes and recreation areas.

A tangle of foliage gives a deliberately unkempt look to this suburban garden. Mature trees provide dappled shade. In the centre is a mature silver birch (*Betula*) (2), popular for its white peeling bark.
● Silver birch grows up to 35ft (11m) high, but compact varieties are also available—for example, the weeping *B. pendula* 'Youngii'.

1 Informal groups of herbs and ground-cover plants	3 Narrow path of paving slabs and bricks	5 Entrance from street
2 Silver birch (*Betula pendula*)	4 False acacia (*Robinia pseudoacacia*)	

An aromatic approach to the house is provided by a variety of herbs such as lemon balm, golden thyme *Artemisia* and rosemary, allowed to sprawl informally at either side of the path. The arching trees frame a view of dark-green cotoneaster.

POINTS OF COLOR

There will always be a place for an unashamedly romantic garden designed to appeal directly to the senses. Here, no attempt has been made to adhere to a strong, hard design based on logic. Instead, the garden is dotted loosely with color—especially pink and red. This approach is reminiscent of the *pointillist* technique of painting, whereby a soft, shimmering picture is built up out of a mass of small dabs.

In such a garden, bold-leaved architectural plants would be out of place. Instead, there is an overall effect of lightness and delicacy. The plants have been chosen for the airy beauty of their flowers. Even the three arches that divide the lawn from the paved area and provide a support for roses are made of thin wire rather than the more usual woodwork.

From early summer to the first frosts, the garden becomes an abundant and fragrant place, with roses spilling everywhere. Afterwards, color is provided by the rose-hips, which flare a rich red, and by leaves in transparent orange and yellow tints.

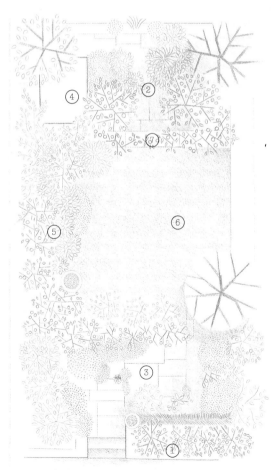

1 Trellis supporting 'Iceberg' rose on house wall

2 Paved area with mixed country garden plants

3 Small paved area with mound-forming plants

4 Garden shed

5 Mixed herbaceous border

6 Small lawn

7 Three wire arches supporting 'Handel' climbing rose

The pink blooms of the fine old 'Handel' rose threaten to overwhelm the supporting arches and almost obliterate the view into the small paved garden beyond, which contains a concealed garden shed. They also wrest attention from the white spires of mallow in the foreground. A more dramatic effect could have been created by using roses of a vivid red, such as 'Kassel'.
● Red or pink flowers in the foreground of a view can be effectively highlighted by placing a delicate sprinkling of blue in the background. Blue is a "receding" color, and tends to give an impression of distance, whereas red seems to advance.

An urn, simply planted with tiny ivy-leaved pelargoniums and white alyssum, stands among a rich surround–gold-eyed tree poppies (*Romneya coulteri*), large red and white peonies and a massive tuft of white bell-flowered, silver-leaved *Convolvulus cneorum*, a beautiful tender shrub.
● Double peonies have a longer season than single ones: popular varieties are pink *P. offinalis* 'Rosea Plena' and pink *P. 'Sarah Bernhardt'*. All peonies need an open, sunny spot, but preferably avoiding the first rays of the sun.

Right **White bells** of *Campanula lactiflora* contrast beautifully with the dark green foliage of the 'Iceberg' rose. The cottage garden atmosphere is emphasized by traditional plants such as the low mound of pink-flowered thrift (*Armeria maritima*), the silver-leaved *Senecio* 'Ramparts' and the cloud of *Gypsophila repens*.

AN L-SHAPED POOL

This garden is so heavily planted around its margins that without the open geometry of the simply paved terrace, and the cool, dark surface of the L-shaped, formal pool, it might have become claustrophobic. Instead, the pool has made it a haven of calm inside a thick palisade of trees and shrubs.

The pool is raised behind a wall, so that its reflections are brought nearer to the eye and make more impact. Goldfish provide movement in lieu of a fountain.

The subtle shades of pinks and grays and regular pattern of the paving slabs create a clean, uncluttered terrace. In contrast, the pool surround is a drystone wall, comprising many different shapes of stone.

The plants surrounding the pool have been specially chosen to present a wide range of textures. The single clump of *Sagittaria sagittifolia*, with its distinctive arrow-shaped heads, provides a sudden vertical element that strongly contrasts with the horizontal line of the water. Marking the corner of the pool is a small clump of marsh marigolds: these are rampant, and need to be carefully controlled. Yellow-flowered *Ligularia* bordering the pool blooms at the same time as the red *Hibiscus rosa-sinensis*.

1 L-shaped pool

2 Raised bed

3 *Sagittaria sagittifolia*

4 *Mahonia nervosa*

5 Table and chairs

6 *Clivia* in pot

7 *Columnea* in pot

8 Lily-flowered tulips for summer color

9 Marsh marigolds (*Caltha palustris*)

10 Path along side of house

Above **In spring,** lily-flowered tulips in white, red and yellow lift their heads on their strong slender stems at the margin of the pool. They have been carefully planted in three distinct blocks of color, though without being regimented.

In summer, the pool nestles amid a spectacular display of greenery and restrained patches of vivid flower color. The red *Columnea* at the corner of the pool (foreground) (7) tones in well with the *Hibiscus rosa-sinensis.* The *Ligularia* at the back sounds a cheerful note. Leaf forms vary from arrow-shaped *Sagittaria* (3), adjacent to a feathery cascade of *Pennisetum orientalis*, to the compound leaves of *Mahonia nervosa* along the left-hand margin (4). Towering above (top left corner of picture) is *Magnolia grandiflora.*

The arching heads of *Pennisetum orientalis*, suggestive of a watery cascade, make an excellent choice of planting for a pool margin. Other suitable plants with a similar habit would be *Carex pendula* or *Helictotrichon sempervirens*.

Delicate verticals distinguish the planting in this part of the pool. Complementing the lily-flowered tulips are upright grasses whose soft textures contrast with the pool surround.

In the shelter afforded by the boundary fence, *Hibiscus rosa-sinensis* puts forth its showy exotic flowers.

● *H. rosa-sinensis* is a deciduous shrub, notable for its pointed dark-green leaves and loose summer flowers, which are vivid but short-lived.

Right **Impatience** tumbles in a mass of white blooms over the pool edge. The *Clivia* in the foreground bears golden-orange flowers in the spring, but is also valued for its striking evergreen, strap-shaped leaves.

GRAND CANAL

The great strength of this design lies in the interesting way in which the materials—heavy timber, gravel, brick and water—have been combined to fully exploit the contrast in their textures. A series of regular geometric shapes of varying colors and textures has been arranged into an abstract asymmetrical pattern with a sense of balance and appropriateness.

Confining the water to an L-shaped canal, set on two levels joined by a dam, and fed from the spout of an old cast-iron pump, is an attractive if somewhat contrived alternative to the more usual styles of garden pool. This arrangement has the merit of introducing a variety of effects—the plunging and burrowing jet from the pump, the ripple as the water moves on along the canal, the placid mirror of the surface above the dam, and the froth as it cascades down. All these different stimuli can be experienced as you linger on the terrace.

A statue at the end of a canal, and wooden bridges crossing it, are features that anyone can incorporate in a modestly-sized garden without difficulty.

Provided that the gravel has been laid over weed-suppressing black plastic sheeting, the maintenance in this garden should be minimal because the planting, except in the graveled area, is sparse. In cold climates, hardier plants could easily be included within the same basic framework.

1 Garden shed

2 Purple smoke tree creates strong color contrast with gravel

3 Ivies and climbers break up monotony of fence

4 Timber slats set into gravel

5 Right-angled canal

6 Mound-forming and trailing plants

7 Miniature dam

8 Yucca in pot

9 Statue

10 Large clump of *Crocosmia crocosmiiflora* near water feature

11 Old-fashioned water pump

12 Wooden bridges

Timber slats set in a base of gravel (4), contrasting with the brickwork and echoing the wooden fence, show the beauty of mixing materials. The chairs can be folded away when not in use.

Above *Agave americana* **and** *Phormium tenax* provide intricately contrasting forms among the broken texture of the pebbles and gravel. The two agaves are 'Marginata' and the smaller 'Medio-picta'.

Left **An old water pump** (11) makes a novel garden artefact.
● When choosing ornamental features such as this, consider their appropriateness to the overall effect. In a small garden with a decidedly modern feel, objects with traditional associations might clash with the prevailing mood.

ORNAMENTAL CHIMNEYPOTS

This courtyard gravel garden has a quiet distinction, thanks to tasteful ornamental details, carefully-selected, rather subdued planting and a fine formal pool whose circular shape is emphasized by the raised surround of slightly separated bricks. The small plume of water tumbling back onto the pool surface provides all the animation that the garden needs.

The most prominent ornamental features are the three chimneypots—good examples of the effectiveness of incorporating detached architectural details into a small garden to give it extra character. Castaway columns or fragments of a classical architrave could be used to similar effect.

Strictly symmetrical, with a constricted "waist" dividing the ornamental area from the utility area, the garden's plan is emphasized by a narrow skirt of lawn, which of course requires some maintenance. To introduce an element of variety, the two chimneypots are of differing design—one with a spiral pattern, the other with a lattice and topped by a grey-leaved succulent in a pot. Partially obscured by greenery is an interwoven wooden fence, capped with a coping of ivy.

The elements of this design could easily be borrowed for either a front or back garden.

1 Garden shed

3 *Senecio compactus* for ground cover

5 Standard roses, *Campanula latifolia* and delphiniums give long-lasting splashes of summer color

7 Pale pink rose

8 Pond edged with bricks

2 Grass edging

4 Ornamental terracotta chimney pots

6 Gravel surface

9 Fountain

10 Wisteria on wall of house

Architectural ornaments can often be used, as here, to support a pot plant. The succulents in the urn on top of this chimneypot will stand any amount of dry weather and are well sited, as they will rarely need watering. To the left of the ornament is a clump of day lilies. Delphiniums nearby provide a muted vertical accent.

Right **The siting** of this ornamental chimneypot helps to divert attention from the garden shed next to it. At the base of the chimney are two varieties of hosta – *H. plantaginea* and *H. crispula* – and yellow-flowered *Senecio compactus*. An 'Iceberg' rose and an evergreen honeysuckle beyond provide contrast to the ornament's strong form.

● Hostas are grown not only for their attractive broad leaves (often variegated) but also for their pale lilac or white flowers produced on tall stems in mid-summer. (This photograph was taken in early summer, prior to flowering.)

WALKING ON WATER

The conviction with which this design aims to create a very special type of pool garden is apparent in the use of first-class materials and great attention to detail. As in many successful small gardens, no attempt has been made to introduce such common garden elements as herbaceous borders or shrubberies. Instead there is a wealth of spectacular and unusual features—a square island of greenery, stone steps joining the two levels, a group of paving stones raking across the pool in pairs, two polygonal trelliswork pavilions, and a fine pergola with a hint of the oriental in its style.

Inventive use is made of timber, which is employed not only for architectural structures and the retaining wall of the bed adjacent to the pool, but also as a decorative coping—for example, around the edge of the lawn.

The planting has been chosen to introduce a broad range of greens and restrained but long-lasting flower color. For example, one of the beds next to the pergola (shown in the photograph, far right) produces a sustained burst of yellow, as the *Euphorbia characias* takes over from the early-flowering *Mahonia japonica* alongside.

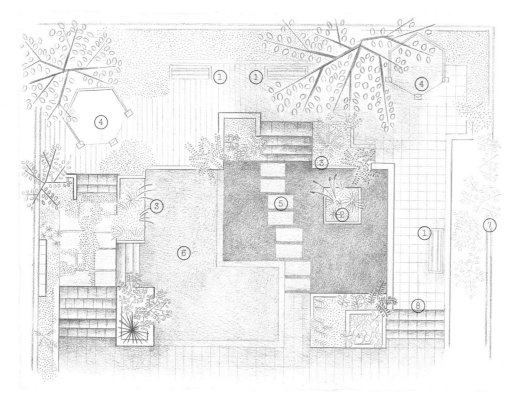

Above Dark slate paving makes a striking transition between the pale stone steps and the wooden deck on which the pavilion stands. The slate slabs have been laid with generous gaps to accommodate a range of mound-forming plants in greens and grays. The arching pale green fronds of *Robinia pseudoacacia* 'Frisia' stand out particularly well against this background. Behind are sword-like leaves of red phormiums.
● As this view shows, slate takes on an attractive, much darker appearance when wet.

1 Wooden benches

2 Island with wooden coping

3 Beds retained by timber slats

4 Pavilions

5 Stepping stones crossing pond

6 Lawn

7 Trellis on brick wall

8 Pergola

Left **The stepping stones**, asymmetrically arranged to prevent the rectilinear plan from being too regular, are in the same clean-cut, high-quality stone as the steps and raised terracing. The timber features provide a variation in color and texture. Doubling as a shed for storage, the custom-built pavilion has a slightly curved conical roof with upturned eaves, recalling Chinese garden architecture.

Above **Reminiscent of a ship's deck**, the pergola has a balustrade from which to peer down into the water. The balustrade's design echoes the triangular motifs on the trellising behind.
● Although in time a structure like this might be festooned with plants, ideally it should look attractive in its bare, skeletal state, as here.

SQUARE POOLS

Including two small water features in a garden, as this design does, is often a better option than a single larger pool, which might seem too dominant in a small plot. To increase the variety of sensations, an island bed of plants that enjoy shade and moisture has been located between the two ponds. The tall astilbes in the bed, located on the not-quite-central axis, arrest attention, preventing the eye from straying to the end of the garden too quickly.

This garden follows the golden rule of formal pool-making: not to obscure the hard edges of a pool with too many overhanging plants. A pond may be either natural-looking or geometric, but if you choose the latter option it is important to have the courage of your convictions.

The planting is profuse and mixed, with an interesting combination of trees, shrubs and aquatic plants providing a variety of foliage and flower types; this makes it difficult to judge the size of the garden at first glance. Container plants provide versatility.

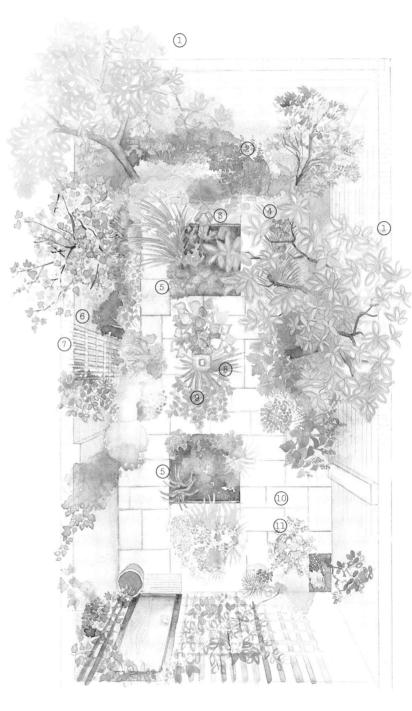

1 Deciduous magnolias

2 Maple

3 Statue of Pan

4 Bearded irises (*I. germanica*)

5 Square pools

6 *Fremontodendron californicum* and spring-flowering *Clematis*

7 Trellis section breaks uniformity of brick wall

8 Bird bath

9 Astilbe

10 Paving of rectangular flags

11 Pot containing white petunias and *Helichrysum petiolatum*

Right **Bearded irises** form a platoon in the foreground. Together with the yellow irises beyond, they provide a fine array of color for a short time early in the season—as does the clematis on the wall. As this color fades, the lilies in the pond will come into bloom. The majestic *Fremontodendron californicum* on the wall, pleasingly entangled with a clematis, will go on offering its giant buttercups until late in the summer. (It is hardy only in warm climates.)
● The most familiar bearded irises are tall (2½ft/1m or more), but dwarf varieties, under 9in (2.5cm), are also available.

Right **Portable color** for a long season is provided by the few white petunias and thriving *Helichrysum petiolatum* that garnish this planting tub. The notion of allowing *Tradescantia* to emerge from a sward of miniature thyme (foreground, left) is well worth copying. Also of interest is the use of dark, variegated ornamental clovers (lower edge of picture). At the rear of the garden, beyond the *Astilbe* and the Japanese anemone (*A.* x *hybrida*), a diminutive statue of Pan acts as a focal point.

A DOUBLE-APSED POOL

An enjoyable design, full of interesting tension, can often be created by using informally-shaped materials to make formal shapes. Here, random paving stones make a sharp contrast with the definite shape of a double-apsed pool. Here and there, gaps have been left in the paving to make room for a few mound-forming rock plants. Dense planting around the edges, with a of evergreens, completes the effect.

The pool is distinguished by a sculptural fountain, with calla lilies for height and water lilies to evoke mystery and calm. The most suitable water lilies for shallow water are *Nymphaea* × *Laydeckeri* varieties, including red 'Purpurata' and white 'Alba'. For deeper water you could choose the large vigorous *N.* × *Marliacea* varieties, the most popular of which is yellow-flowered 'Chromatella'. Other planting choices for a pond like this might include water starwort (*Callitriche*) and hornwort (*Ceratophyllum*), which have pretty foliage and are easy to control.

Simplicity and good proportions are the essence of this design. The trouble it took to give the pond rounded ends has been well justified by the results.

1 Water lilies in double-apsed pond

2 Three shallow steps

3 Fragrant tobacco plant (*Nicotiana*) and herbs surrounding seating area

4 Rock plants in gaps between crazy paving

5 Decorative stone seat

6 Raised patio area

7 Sculptural fountain (see page 79)

A stone seat resting on sculpted gryphons conforms with the general formality of the setting. The cold stone of the seat is not so much intended for use, as to draw the visitor's attention to the area. *Dianthus caryophyllus* creates a red color accent in a gap between the paving stones. To the right of this view are the tall, white trumpets of the calla lily (*Zantedischia aethiopeca*) standing ankle-deep in the water.

● Marginal plants such as these calla lilies make no contribution to the balance of the pool but earn their place by virtue of their ornamental value. Keep varieties within the pool in separate containers, or they will compete and the most vigorous will choke the rest.

High-quality pots like these terracotta ones are an essential ingredient in a formal garden. Here, they hold *Euonymus fortunei*, with its attractive variegated leaves, and red-berried *Solanum capsicastrum*. A sympathetic background is provided by a variegated Virginia creeper (*Parthenocissus henryana*).

Resemblances between plants and ornaments can often be effective. Here, the trumpets of arum lilies perfectly complement the horn-blowing statue-fountain. The small water lilies, 'Froebeli', with deep red blooms, are free-flowering—an ideal choice for a medium-sized pool.

Above **This alpine composition** includes *Arabis hispanica*, pale green *Sedum spathalafolium*, a mound of saxifrage and, around the base of the rock, ivy-leaved toadflax (*Cymbalaria muralis*).
● Saxifrages, a large group, form evergreen mats or carpets. They produce small rounded flowers in spring, in red, pink, yellow or white.

A POOL TO RELAX BY

In regions of abundant sunshine and warmth, often the most satisfying option is to devote the available garden space to a swimming pool, with an appealing surround.

The key to success with a garden dominated by a pool is to use high-quality materials and refrain from putting in the usual jazzy pool accoutrements. Complementary poolside plants should be carefully chosen.

It is tempting to beautify the area with lovely flowering plants, such as fragrant lavender, but you must take the conditions into account. Swimming pool water is a precisely controlled chemical solution, which in order to remain safe has to be sterilized and constantly filtered. Fine plant seeds in the water are likely to block the filtration system of the pool and, because they are organic, they reduce the chlorine level very quickly.

The rule, therefore, is to choose evergreens such as yuccas, bamboos, camellias, euonymus, hebes, laurels, oleanders and santolinas. All these make excellent poolside plants because they lose their leaves slowly, their flowers are persistent and they hold onto their seeds for a long time after the flowers have faded—giving you time to "dead-head" with clippers.

1 Evergreens in brick-retained bed

2 Sheltered area for barbecue and storage

3 Bamboo surrounded by rocks and boulders

4 Timber decking: comfortable to walk on barefooted, provides good drainage

5 Planting in tubs keeps soil out of pool

6 Phormium tenax

7 Japanese maple

Above **A Japanese maple** (7) and a yucca in large tubs provide foliage interest. The large boulders (counterpointed by the smaller ones in the near pot) give added visual weight; the pots might otherwise have seemed isolated. Indicating a route, the mat serves a visual as well as a practical purpose.

Below **A raised border** alongside the house (1) is strengthened by a potted *Cyperus*. Just visible here are spotlights sunk into the border, providing attractive effects for a night-time swim. For safety reasons, it is essential to have good lighting around swimming pools.

The comfortable timbers that surround the pool are reminiscent of a ship's deck. They create additional interest by being set at different levels and various angles to the pool margin. They are wide enough apart to allow for rapid drainage. The striped, strap-like leaves of the potted phormium (6) in the foreground provide a pleasing contrast, in structure and color, to the delicate fronds of bamboo (3).

● To prevent soil from spilling into the pool, it is a good idea to coat the planted surface with rocks and coarse pebbles to hold the soil in place. Here, the rocks and boulders in three different sizes create a sculptural still-life.

● A swimming pool with a blue lining is attractive in a warm climate but can look cold and obtrusive under northern skies. In temperate zones, a warmer-colored lining looks more natural.

SYMMETRY AND ILLUSION

A simple, symmetrical treatment of water can be pleasing, provided that the scale and proportions are correctly judged. Here, with great audacity, the designer has made a short canal running down the garden along its central axis. The impact of the water has been visually extended by stationing a panel of outdoor-grade mirror at the far end of the canal, which thus appears to flow beyond the trelliswork boundary. The mirror also duplicates a pot of irises, which half-conceals a waterspout set into its silvered surface. The effect of the mirror is not only to deceive the eye, but also to spread light in the garden, creating a sunny patch in an area of shade.

The rectangle of water is framed in a formal brick terrace, without any transitional surround. This brickwork too is rigidly symmetrical, in the form of a cross, with container plants to alleviate the monotony.

Either side of the mirror, the square-section trellis is tightly spaced, which gives it a shimmering effect—a technique highly appropriate in a garden that makes use of optical illusion.

Here and there are classical touches which give the garden a feeling of elegance and tradition—for example, the urns posted at either side of the steps up to the house (shown in the photograph opposite) and the twin stone pineapples that mark the corners of the raised beds. One of these pineapples, stationed next to a clump of lavender, is just visible in the picture below.

Smooth stones scattered on the pool bottom more than compensate for the lack of planting. As the water is in constant motion, via a waterspout projecting from the mirror end and a disguised outlet at the opposite end, there is no need for oxygenating plants.

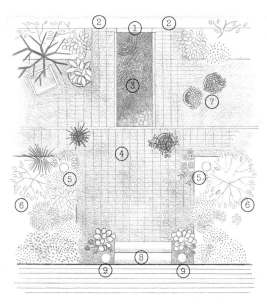

4 Brick terrace

5 Stone pineapples

6 Architectural planting in raised beds

7 Matching movable pots of white pelargoniums

8 Steps to veranda flanked by urns containing bergenia and trailing lobelia

9 Ivy-covered pillars

1 Mirror enlarges apparent length of pool with a decorative waterspout set into the mirror

2 Square-section trellis

3 Canal-like pond scattered with smooth stones

Left **Ivy** has transformed a simple wooden veranda post into an evocative garden feature. The veranda provides shady conditions for a potted fern. In matching urns either side of the steps mounted on bricks for extra height, rich dark-dreen bergenia leaves provide a plain background to the starry white trailing lobelia. The brickwork shows a blend of pale and dark tones combined to form a random pattern.
● The exuberance of ivy and other rampant climbers should be curbed when they reach the roof line: otherwise they will crawl under the roof and damage the tiles or shingles.

Above **A silvery-green tumble** of *Alyssum saxatile* sits well with the yellow-flowered *Ruta graveolens* and large-leaved *Anemone* x *hybrida*.

INTERLOCKING POOLS

Two grand piano-shaped ponds, divided by a marsh area and a brick walkway, form the centerpiece of this garden. Both ponds are dark and mysterious, and planted principally with water lilies. Straight stone slabs serving as coping along the edges of the ponds contrast with the serpentine shape of the brick path. Ferns, irises and other damp-loving plants, including wood violets, enjoy the humid conditions in the intermediate marsh area.

The enclosure, effectively defending the garden from prying eyes beyond, is also highly distinctive. High trellis panels of unusual design serve as ramparts on top of a whitewashed brick wall. Similar trellis work has been used to cover a novel circular window, like a notional sun, cut into an arched brick insert (shown in the photograph, far right)—a personalized feature which gives the garden a stamp of real style. Much thought has also been given to the paving, dominated by the charming, herringbone-patterned, weathered brickwork.

Most of the trees and shrubs are informally planted in beds at the foot of the walls. They include such pleasingly simple plants as the white-flowered buddleia and the giant strap-leaved red *Phormium tenax*, dominating one of the far corners. The substantial garden shed, sited in the other far corner, is stained dark brown, with a dull black roof, making it satisfactorily unobtrusive.

Excellently scaled and shaped, this garden is simple yet full of interest, offering great freedom of movement within a small area. Splashes of flower color—especially red—show up well against the predominantly green background.

1 Arched insert with trellised window

2 Complementary-shaped pools edged with petunias and zonal pelargoniums for annual color

3 Intermediate marsh area

4 Weathered brick in herringbone pattern

5 New Zealand flax (*Phormium tenax*)

6 Trellis above brick wall increases seclusion

7 Curved brick walkway separates the two pools

8 Shallow step

9 Buddleia

10 Hydrangea

Above **A shallow step** (8) in the curving brick path slows down the pace as one walks through the garden, drawing attention to the mixed textures of plants in the marsh area (2). As this example shows, even slight changes of level can make a strong impact if they create a distinct band of shadow. The zonal pelargoniums add splashes of scarlet, supported by purple petunias. To the left in this picture is a clump of day lilies (*Hemerocallis*), seen here in an interval between flowerings; these will grow in any moisture-retaining soil. Hybrids come in a vast range of flower colors.
● Duckweed, whose tiny leaves add carpets of green to this pool, can be bothersomely prolific. But if you are prepared to control it by regular scooping, moderate quantities of duckweed can look attractive, especially in a pool lined with mat black materials.

Left **A white butterfly bush**, *Buddleia davidii* (9), contrasts with hydrangeas in the border alongside the dining terrace.
● Buddleias are quick-growing. They are too often spoiled by neglect: you need to prune hard in early spring.

Above **The trellised "sun"** (1) is an eye-catching feature, beyond an area of planting which is itself full of interest— including the tall *Abutilon* flanking the circle.
● Trelliswork usually has a simple diamond or square pattern, but it is worth looking for more unusual patterns. Here, double and triple slats increase seclusion.

POOLS ON TWO LEVELS

A garden planned on a rectilinear grid can often be made more interesting if the grid is angled in relation to the house and boundaries. This is the approach taken here. The dominant feature of interest is a split-level pool, turned at 45°, whose impact can be enjoyed from a spacious dining terrace.

Placing the L-shaped part of the pool above ground level, produces an effect of agreeable surprise, bringing both the water surface and the planting closer to the eye.

The plants are an informal jumble, in contrast to the simple, uncluttered paving area. There are plenty of colorful annuals, such as the bright red geraniums and nasturtiums that spill freely over the clean lines of the raised bed wall. As well as evergreens to provide an all-year structure of green, the garden includes roses and a hydrangea, whose flowers appear especially vivid against the light-colored paving.

1 Trellis

2 Hydrangea

3 Uncluttered seating area

4 Raised beds retained by stone walls

5 Mixed shrubs bordering pool

6 Split-level interlocking pools

7 Light-colored paving stones

8 Small fountain

Left **Shrubs**, like the large-leaved false castor oil plant (*Fatsia japonica*) and the sprawling *Juniperus horizontalis*, soon fuse together to form a varied shrubbery. The small area of soil exposed at the edge of the bed has allowed room for annuals, such as nasturtiums. The heron is one of a pair, the other one placed prominently in the angle of the upper pool (see photograph opposite).

Left **Aquatic plants** require little maintenance, but because they flourish in summer and die back in winter, they lend the same kind of seasonal excitement as that provided by herbaceous beds. Behind the raised bed, a trellis fence of white squares enlivens the brick boundary wall.

● A fountain, besides being ornamental, improves the oxygenation of the water in warm weather.

● As an alternative to the ubiquitous water lilies, there are various other aquatic plants you could choose. Examples are water hyacinth (*Eichhomia crassipes*, which floats on the surface, or deep-water plants such as yellow-flowering *Nuphar lutea* or white-flowering water hawthorn (*Aponogeton distachyus*).

A MINIATURE CLIFF

All the classic elements of a suburban plot— lawn, shrubs and herbaceous beds—are thoughtfully combined in this garden, and the quality of the planting is high. A notable feature is the high-level walkway running along one of the boundary walls; although paved with old bricks, its side wall is of rugged masonry, like a miniature cliff (see the photograph on page 90). At the foot of the wall, and growing in pockets between the masonry, male ferns (*Dryopteris Filix-mas*) help to create a wilderness effect. Nestling among them at ground level is a niche containing a striking classical bust—the kind of surprise feature that works particularly well in a garden dominated by a wealth of informal planting.

Such surprises can be contrived even in the smallest of plots.

The lawn is given added interest by its discreetly irregular shape and its division by a deep and attractive stone step.

The well-established wall of fine old bricks emanates a feeling of mellowness, seclusion and calm, and this has been deliberately enhanced by leaving certain parts of the wall exposed, the rest concealed by intermittent climbing plants which prevent any impression of monotony.

The woodland area at the end of the garden is backed by a thick, clipped hedge, just over 6ft (2m) high, which serves as an effective screen and natural boundary.

1 Ornamental niche with bust see page 91)

2 Raised walkway with pot plants

3 Brick wall with climbers

4 Steps joining lawn with raised walkway

5 Lush informal planting

6 Climbers on improvised wooden framework

7 Low clipped hedge marks rear boundary

8 Deep stone step in lawn

9 Wide herbaceous borders and irregularly shaped lawn create balanced composition

A raised walkway (2) leading from the house provides a viewpoint from which to look down into the rest of the garden. The logs and stone ornaments help to convey a deliberate sense of jumble. The brickwork has been softened but not obliterated by the festoon of climbers, which thrive in the warmth and protection of a high brick wall.

A stone step (8) in the lawn divides the border at the right from a miniature island bed containing yellow *Alyssum saxatile*. At the other side of the bed, to the left of this view, a gentle slope in the lawn gives easy access to the lower level for a mower. ● A popular rock plant, *Alyssum saxatile* is easy to grow in a sunny open spot. Its golden-yellow flowers appear in spring. For the smaller plot, there is a dwarf variety that grows to only 6in (15cm)

Left **Broad shields** of *Hosta sieboldiana* and outstretched palms of *Helleborus corsicus* contrast well with tall spears of the day lily (*Hemerocallis*) and the variegated ivy that trails down from the wall behind. A cascade of sedge grass (*Carex pendula*) completes the composition.

Far left **The hedge** at the foot of the garden has been clipped low enough to welcome a view of mature trees beyond. The stair rail supports a sprawling mass of asters, adding to the informality of the scene.

Left **Brickwork and stone** work harmoniously together in this garden, serving as hosts to a variety of planting. Adding an accent of yellow to the brick boundary wall is another clump of *Alyssum saxatile* (see also page 89).

Above **Ferns, bamboo,** a clump of hardy geraniums and *Hyacinthus hispanicus* form a miniature woodland scene surrounding a niche in the rugged masonry wall of the raised walkway. The coy-looking bust of a lady provides an effective focus of interest.

● Small statues or busts of this kind do not need an elevated position to earn their worth: instead, you can use them at ground level, half-concealing them by flowers or greenery to make a virtue of obscurity. In this example, note the effective contrast of the bust's whiteness against the dark niche.

A PATHWAY OF SQUARES

An L-shaped plot, far from being a problem, has an immediate advantage in design terms, providing opportunities for surprise effects. In this attractive town garden, extra interest is created by having the two arms of the L at different levels. The dining terrace is located in the sunken area, out of view from the house, encouraging the feeling of moving into a different world. The high fencing, serving as a backdrop for plants, makes an efficient windbreak and creates a sense of intimacy.

Paving slabs of the same type have been used for both halves of the garden. However, in the dining terrace they are laid in a simple grid pattern; whereas nearer the house they are in alternating rows, with a distinctly dogleg effect. Between the slabs, lines of smaller paving units define the pattern.

Looking toward the house, the strong sculptural form of the spiral staircase makes a major impact.

1 Painted shadow on fence

2 Crabapple trees

3 Seating area out of view from the house

4 Paving slabs in a grid pattern

5 Evergreen *Mahonia japonica*

6 Massed tulips for spring color

7 Unplanted ornamental vase

8 Shallow flight of steps

The three steps that separate the two halves of the garden produce an exciting change of viewpoint in the view back towards the house. The pot on the end of one of the brick flanking walls introduces an eyecatching vertical feature.
● One way to give extra emphasis to a structural feature is to use a material that is absent elsewhere in the garden, or is used only in small details. Here, the flanking walls are all the more distinctive for being the only features in red brick.

Right **Framing large paving slabs** with smaller brick-sized units makes what could otherwise have been an uninteresting hard surface into a subtle feature. Note how the smaller units, in pairs with a narrow strip between, repeat the larger pattern in which they are contained. Just noticeable on the rear fence (behind the tree) is a clever *trompe l'oeil* effect: a painted shadow which gives the illusion of sunlight even on a dull day.

Right **Tulips** massed together provide a bold display of early color to make the winter feel shorter. After their petals have fallen, an ornamental crabapple will fill this corner of the garden with delicate blossom. At the foot of the steps in the corner of the bed is early-flowering *Mahonia*, whose leaves will add greenery all year.

STEPS ON THE CENTRAL AXIS

Interesting effects can be achieved in a split-level garden by turning the steps at right angles to the main axis instead of across the plot in the more conventional way.

Here, steps following this arrangement are used to link two paved areas based on interlocking L-shapes. The steps stretch between two raised beds running out from opposite walls toward the center of the plot, at different distances from the house. These beds are filled with evergreens, which serve as screens shielding the back area of the garden from the front. An arbor with an attractive cast-iron seat provides a shady place to enjoy the scent of climbers. Continuity is given by the use of a similar style of high-quality white-painted furniture in the foreground.

Despite its simplicity, this is a garden of considerable originality, in which every aspect of the planning is carefully considered to make maximum use of available space.

A feeling of intimacy has been reinforced by shrouding the boundary fence and wall almost completely in plants. When stone is such a dominant feature, it should be of high quality and preferably well-weathered, as it is here.

The paving material in this garden is expensive quarried stone. A less costly option, but one which requires more maintenance, would be to lay a closely cropped lawn. This could extend the whole length of the space, or be confined to the back half, thus offering a place to spread out and sunbathe, as an alternative to the more "refined" paved seating area.

1 Thick evergreen planting obscures far boundary

2 White cast-iron bench sheltered by arbor

3 Urns containing annuals

4 Evergreen beds act as screens

5 Shallow steps

6 Garden furniture

Evergreens, including the mature, beautifully rounded bay tree, the shrubby, unpruned rosemary bush and the pyramid-shaped *Picea alberti* 'Comica', serve as the garden's "upholstery", their predominantly dark green color beautifully setting off the color and form of the flowers. The herbaceous perennials, such as the white lupines, pink peonies and climbers–roses and clematis–provide summer color.

Above left **The garden seat** (2) in the area farther from the house is attractively framed in a plant-covered arbor.
● Such arbors are easy to make out of old timber. If you cover the frame with fast-growing climbers, you need not worry too much about the quality of the workmanship. Scented climbers are particularly apt for such a position.

Left **An urn** accommodating petunias and white *Nicotiana alata* is grouped with large-flowered clematis 'Comtesse de Bouvard' and bamboo.

Above **Peonies and a grapevine** frame this view of the white table on which a potted pink fuchsia stands. Beyond, among other plants, are lupins, a standard bay tree (*Laurus novilis*) and pink roses.
● In temperate zones bay trees need to be over-wintered under glass.

95

TRELLIS TRACERY

In this intriguing split-level garden, the interest has been increased by a relatively complex plan. The well-defined lower and upper terraces are both pleasingly asymmetrical in form. Linking the two levels, a flight of steps follows the curving retaining wall of a raised bed.

The forbidding high brick end wall of the garden has been effectively subdued by giving it a light color wash and attaching unusual arched trellising, and brackets from which planted baskets hang. Continuity is maintained by using the same trellising on two of the other walls. On the upper terrace, white-painted decorative furniture adds a finishing touch.

1 Arched trellis design against pale green wall makes space seem larger

2 Hanging baskets with fuchsias

3 Wall shrubs in brick-retained raised beds

4 Curved brick staircase

5 Brick pillar supporting annuals around a small water basin

6 Sheltered lower terrace

Above **The pastel green** of the walls enhances the foliage and the white trellis work–a suitable alternative to whitewashed walls which tend to look rather bleak and rapidly become dirty. The trellis provides good accommodation for an interesting range of plants that will flourish in shade.
● Variegated ivies such as 'Goldheart' and 'Tricolor' will do well in such shady places. Other suitable plants for the trellis might include climbing hydrangea (*Hydrangea petiolaris*) or winter jasmine (*Jasminum nudiflorum*).

Right **Two kinds of annual**, thickly planted–*Begonia semperflorens* and trailing lobelia–make a cheerful eyecatching natural banister for the flight of steps. The plants are arranged around a small basin of water from which a tiny lead statue rises.

LIGHT AT THE END OF THE TUNNEL

An L-shaped plot is an asset in planting because it offers two distinct vistas. There is always a mystery area around the corner, which makes it impossible to judge, at a glance, the real extent of the garden. These advantages are particularly precious in a tiny garden such as this.

Additional interest has been created by exploiting two levels, linked by a broad flight of steps that runs along one of the side walls. The walls and pots have been used to great effect to support a remarkable number of plants.

The creepers, arching toward each other across the arm of the L that is nearer the house, make a kind of leafy tunnel which filters the sunlight and throws attractive shadows. This effect does much to increase the feeling of depth in a small garden. In a shady plot such as this, vivid features such as the yellow chairs used here prevent too gloomy an effect. The upper level is more open, providing a seating area where, on a sunny day, there is an option of sun or shade.

The bricks used for the paving have been laid in different patterns on the stairs and the flat terraced areas—as can be seen by comparing the photograph below with those on the opposite page. Such niceties of design are all-important in creating an impression of quality.

1 White-painted diamond trellis

2 Raised seating area with yellow chairs and glass-topped table

3 Pot plants on stairs create tiers of color

4 Climbers give effect of a leafy tunnel

5 Good-quality brickwork

Right **A bright chair** has been strategically sited to lure the eye along the leafy tunnel and up the steps. In the foreground are daisies and *Chrysanthemum maximum*, evergreen *Euonymus fortunei* and *Nicotiana alata* (the latter not yet in flower). A red rose adds bright color along the wall.
● While obviously providing comfortable seating, furniture with soft upholstery has to be chosen with care. If storage space is limited, be sure that the cushions are detachable, so that the chairs themselves can be left outdoors.

Far right **Impatience**, which tolerates partial shade, has been planted in pots, offering flowers over a long season (3).
● Steps such as these make excellent locations for container plants. When planning the dimensions of steps, take into account whether you will want to use them in this way.

Left **A formal terraced area** benefits from the subtle patterns cast by profuse foliage.

CASCADES OF COLOR

With a blaze of color, this garden triumphs over the limitations imposed by a square plot and poor-quality soil.

The emphasis is on rhododendrons, azaleas and other plants for an acid soil. To ensure the right conditions for healthy root development, they have been isolated in deep raised beds filled with a specially-prepared compost mixture containing a high level of peat. Set at different levels in a series of audacious stepped cliffs, these generous growing areas have been used to create an intriguing stone wallscape. The beds have been planned asymmetrically and are never boring. The heavy planting prevents the imposing masonry from being too dominant, and the luxuriously thick foliage ensures that anyone standing in the garden will enjoy a real sense of seclusion. This impression has been reinforced by extending the height of the end fence with a panel of trellising to support climbers.

Although many of the shrubs chosen make their most exciting display in late spring and early summer, there are plenty of subjects which will color wonderfully in the fall, such as the large Japanese maple. At its foot is *Enkianthus*, noted for its flaming fall foliage; and beside it a witch hazel (*Hamamelis*), which bears sweet-scented flowers in winter.

The low beds around the central sitting area allow just enough space for annual and perennial herbaceous plants to provide summer brightness without involving the gardener in too much work. Extra color could be provided by a summer and early autumn show of plants in movable containers. For example, pairs of attractive vases could be stationed on either side of the steps leading to the sitting area.

1 Trellis with climbers

2 Raised bed shown without planting to indicate basic structure

3 Raised beds at different levels

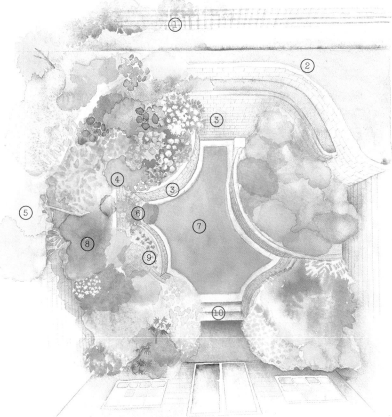

4 Azaleas and other shrubs

5 Japanese maple for fall leaf color

6 Camellia

7 Lawn

8 Witch hazel

9 African marigolds for summer color

10 Steps leading up to sitting area

Single groups of azaleas used almost as polychrome sculpture create a stunning effect. The shiny green leaves and crimson flowers of the camellia (6) add to the impact in spring, while annuals (including marigolds, 9) provide summer color. The golden maple offers a permanent impression of sunshine, and with the scented lilac and variegated ivy helps to soften the perimeter walls.

● Usually daintier than garden rhododendrons, azaleas require acid soil and thrive best in a sheltered, partially shaded spot. Evergreen varieties, which are low and spreading, have distinctive foliage which continues to supply interest after the flowers have dried. Deciduous azaleas grow taller; their blooms are followed by attractive fall leaf color.

SPLASHES OF SILVER

The small scale of this L-shaped basement patio garden is camouflaged by dense planting around its peripheries and the use of accents that divert attention, providing punctuation for the eye as it reads its way around the space.

The change in level makes the available space much more interesting. The central feature is a fountain, offset at an angle to the long axis, and serving as a pivot around which the whole design seems to revolve. The circular vase from which the fountain stems is all the more striking for being set on a square base: superimposing a circle on a square like this is one of the most effective garden design strategies.

Prominent on the upper terrace is a statue—the next resting place for the eye after it has lingered on the vase. The figure is smaller than lifesize, which has the effect of making the garden seem deceptively larger.

1 Predominantly white-flowered and silver foliage plants

2 Graceful statue of nymph creates a focal point

3 Vase-shaped fountain, pivoted at an angle

4 Small pyramid-shaped conifer provides a vertical element

5 Massed impatience decorates the steps

6 Terrace and seating area

7 White brick wall adorned with annuals and climbers

A classical-style fountain will bring life to any garden, and look striking even when turned off. This one is carefully positioned at a change in level, as a kind of psychological newel post to the stairs. The retaining walls at either side are twisted around at the same angle, to emphasize the tension between two different axes. Neighboring plants include exquisite daisies grown in gaps between the paving, pink impatience and *Sagittaria latifolia*.

Delicate fronds of silvery *Artemisia arborescens*, feathery and fragrant, conform to the elegant style of the statue, which is shrouded by bolder planting at its base—for example, variegated hostas. A mixture of fragrant climbers such as the flowering honeysuckle, a clematis and roses help to mask the brick walls, while a framework of mature conifers, including cypress, screen the rear part of the garden from the prying eyes of neighbouring houses.

● The planting around the statue illustrates a useful rule for planting: use delicate foliage at a higher level, and bolder, more emphatic foliage at a lower level.

A STONE GLADE

This small garden in a simple rectangular space offers a wealth of different experiences thanks to a brilliant design based on interlocking curves and dramatic changes of level. The costly excavation and paving materials are justified by the impressive overall effect, which is augmented by rich, thoughtful planting throughout the garden.

The design is an intricate one based on a winding circulation route. A raised path and generous, curved flight of steps lead down from the house door to a low, sheltered dining terrace. From here a longer flight of steps, curving in the opposite direction, leads up to a terraced circular plateau. The random paving here is softened by a scattering of mound-forming plants, shown in the photograph on the opposite page (bottom).

Adjacent to the dining terrace and backed by tiers of raised beds is a semi-circular pool—the hub of the garden. Stepping down either flight of steps into the central area is rather like entering a stone glade. The green amphitheater-like effect around the upper terrace is obtained by planting taller and taller species as the outer walls are approached.

All the masonry, including the paving on the terraces, the steps and the coping of the weather-beaten brick walls that retain the central and peripheral raised beds, has been carried out in the same high-quality stone. This further unifies the design. On the upper terrace a simple seat of stone slabs blends in well with drystone walls on either side. The animal sculptures (opposite, bottom)—a pair of shy fawn-like creatures—are appropriate to the enclosed, secretive mood of this garden. Sculpted human figures would have conveyed a totally different atmosphere.

1 Stone seat on upper terrace backed by dense foliage and flanked by drystone walls

2 Pair of matching stone plant containers

3 Steps up from dining terrace to random-paved plateau

4 Tiered beds

5 Small-scaled pond with aquatic plants

6 Steps down from house to dining terrace

7 Ferns and shade-loving plants in alcove formed by curved flight of steps

Above **The fleshy leaves** of a single *Hosta Fortuneii* 'Aureo-marginata' (7), contrasting with the background stone, announce the beginning of the flight of steps leading to the house.

Right **Sculpted animals** on the alert are enclosed on all sides by rich planting—including a white-flowered broom and (to the right of the picture) a thick cladding of *Clematis montana* and lovely old rose. In the foreground are sharp blades of *Phormium tenax* 'Rainbow'. Note the drystone walls at either side of the seat (1).

Above **The tiny pond** (5) draws our attention like a dark mirror in the heart of the garden. Beyond it, the tiered, raised beds (4), with a purple *Acer palmatum* and yellow broom (*Genista lydia*), act like another flight of steps to be ascended in the mind. Spires of *Primula denticulata* below the vase offer a foil to the potted fuchsia (left.)

RAPID RESULTS

One of the strengths of this stylish terraced garden is the change in level via brick steps. Soil removed from the graveled area has been used to fill the raised beds. The intimacy of the low terrace and the brighter exposure of the second tier offer two distinct experiences. The change in level also helps to keep the eye focused down on the garden, avoiding the feeling of being overlooked by neighbors.

The steps are wide enough to avoid giving the garden a narrow, channeled effect, and to provide a convenient surface for pots. The lower level is paved with gravel, through which a scattering of plants has been grown. A slightly raised brick step makes an interesting divide in the graveled area.

The consistent use of brick throughout the garden has demanded strong planting. Two weeping willows give this angular garden a softness.

The planting follows the principle of using fast-growing plants for rapid results while the more permanent framework of plants slowly establishes itself. In summer the white-flowered *Nicotiana alata* provides lovely fragrance. A winter-flowering cherry bestows color at the bleakest time of year.

1 Raised concrete terrace

2 Weeping willows

3 Raised bed with eucalyptus, rosemary, ceanothus, *Euphorbia Wulfenii* and various annuals

4 Broad brick steps

5 *Rheum palmatum*

6 Raised bed with winter-flowering cherry, *Choisya ternata*, purple sage, *Sedum spectabile* and *Nicotiana alata*

7 Gravel area divided by low brick step

8 Table and chairs

Above right A weeping willow provides a parasol above the seating area. *Nicotiana* helps to conceal pipework. The planting in the raised bed includes more white *Nicotiana*, with red petunias. At the end farthest from the house, the yellow flower heads and spiky leaves of *Euphorbia Wulfenii* blend with *Hydrangea macrophylla*.

Right Purple sage (*Salvia officinalis* 'Purpurea') and *Sedum spectabile* tumble together at the foot of the steps (6).
● Purple sage is one of many herbaceous salvias, related to the kitchen sage. All are fuzzy-leaved and fragrant, with spikes of hooded flowers. Best-known is *Salvia superba*, with violet flower heads 3 feet (1m) high.

One edge of the steps (4) is shrouded in flowers and foliage, some overhanging from the raised bed, others in containers which leave just a narrow passageway for one person at the right-hand side. At the upper level, potted yuccas dominate. The gray foliage of *Stachys lanata* is conspicuous along the front edge of the bed.

A VIEW OF THE SEASHORE

Any garden, however small it may be, will always seem roomy if a view over a landscape as spectacular as this can be "borrowed" and incorporated into the overall design. It is preferable to allow such views to dominate, refraining from fussy planting schemes which would compete with the natural beauty of the scenery.

Wooden decking and wooden fencing have been used to echo the construction of the shingled house (shown on pages 110–11). Timber is perhaps the most natural-looking surfacing medium and is especially pleasing in a rural or seaside setting. It is ideally suited to regions which have an extreme climate–long hot summers, and snow covering the ground for long periods in winter. In damp, temperate climates, wood has a tendency to become too mossy and slippery.

Redwood, cedar and cypress are the most durable woods for decking. Any other constructional timber, such as pine, can be used but will need a special pressure treatment: otherwise, preservatives simply do not penetrate deeply enough. For good drainage, gaps must be left between the planks. Here, spaces have been made in the surface of the decking to allow room for mature trees.

Generally, plants for seaside gardens need to be wind-resistant and tolerant to sand and salt. They must also be capable of growing in very freely drained soils. Good examples are *Escallonia, Fuschia magellicana, Hydrangea macrophylla* and *Senecio*.

1 Hammock adds a note of informality

2 Raised timber decking

3 Gaps in decking allow trees to grow through and soften the hard surface

4 Groups of wind-resistant pot plants

5 Mature trees: *Picea breweriana* (left) and *Arbutus* (right)

6 Specimen plants in large pots

7 Wooden fence low enough to give view over sea

8 Informal seating– wooden benches and tables

Right **An open site** such as this, without access to good soil, is suitable for pot plants that are tolerant of being buffeted by the wind. The simple furniture and the hammock enhance the well-integrated design. Various annuals such as impatience, pansies and white- and pink-flowering gerbera are grouped around purple-leaved *Berberis* x *ottawensis*, a weeping hazel (*Coryllus avellana*) and, tallest of all, *Cupressus cashmeriana*.
● The decking here is built up on joists and beams. Timber decking may also be used at ground level in frost-free climates, so long as provision is made for air to circulate underneath. You can buy commercially made square sections, which are easier to install.

Above, top **Clumps** of wind-resistant *Festuca glauca* grass and ivies balance on the fence, marking the boundary of the garden.

Above **Ornamental seashells**, locally collected, combine with potted thrift (*Armeria maritima*) and club moss to add a touch of style.
● The club moss (*Selginella lycopodioides*) is a "primitive plant": in a peaty soil, given plenty of water, it is virtually indestructible.

Right **A stately spire** of *Acanthus mollis* makes a well-sited bold feature, providing interest at the base of the tree.
● Acanthus is usually regarded as a classical element of a herbaceous border. However, its large, deep-glossy-green, lobed leaves and white flowers held on pinkish-purple bracts can be appreciated best when it is strategically sited as a specimen plant, as here.

Above **A jumble** of miscellaneous pot-grown plants grouped in the center of the deck serves the same purpose as a mixed bed in an inland garden. Included in the composition are large-leaved gerbera, red-flowered *Dianthus barbatus* and the distinctive flower heads of lavender. The weeping hazel (center right) helps to anchor the arrangement

PATIO PROFUSION

The designer's intention when planning a garden in this tiny space was clearly to produce a giant cornucopia—a riot of scented foliage and flowers. Looking into the garden from the house in summer provokes a feeling of natural gaiety, whilst a curved wooden bench only perceptible from within the garden invites pause for quiet reflection or retreat.

Nearly every square foot of wall or ground surface is used to carry a plant of some kind. Trellised walls support a froth of climbers; and all kinds of pots, planters and high-standing jardinieres thrust flowers toward the observer.

As a classic background to the planting, the woven fence and the brick wall of the house have been given a coat of white paint.

1 Single-flowered pelargoniums in pots add splashes of red

2 White-painted walls

3 Curved bench

4 Trellis

5 Spotted laurel (_Aucuba japonica_)

Above **Single pelargoniums** (1) supply splashes of vivid red against a foliage background of spotted laural (*Aucuba japonica*).
● Aucubas are easy to grow in moderate climates. Because they tolerate dense shade, they are well suited to shady courtyards, although the spotted varieties need some sunlight to preserve their yellow leaf markings. Female plants will bear red berries if there is a male nearby.

Right **Petunias**, pelargoniums, chrysanthemums and tobacco plants provide a mass of color and scent.
● Just a few tobacco plants (*Nicotiana alata*) in pots will fill the evening air with an almost inebriating fragrance.
● Pot chrysanthemums are useful to brighten up an area such as this. They can be bought, in flower, at little expense, and offer color for several weeks.

HIGH CHIC

An unashamedly contemporary garden which perfectly matches, in style and detail, the architecture of the house. Painstaking efforts have been made to ensure that the different elements of the garden are in harmony. The pervading feeling is one of "high chic".

The clean lines of the black metal furniture echo those of the framework of the patio door. In the same way, the black color scheme is recapitulated in the style of the plain fence paneling (far right) and black plant pots. The plain brick of the terracing has been chosen to match the house walls.

The designer has opted for relatively sparse but theatrical planting. The huge hogweed (*Heracleum Mantegazzianum*), with its highly architectural form, introduces a strong vertical feature. Gardeners planning to imitate this idea should be reminded that hogweed should not be touched with bare hands, because it is capable of provoking a serious skin rash.

Although the garden is predominantly green, flower color is provided by the potted *Clivia* (bright orange, spring), marguerites (summer) and *Bidens* (yellow, late summer).

This design is disciplined, yet highly individualistic in style. There is a marvellous sense of logical calm. Easily maintained, the garden would perfectly meet the requirements of a busy professional person.

1 Lilies in tubs
  guard doors

2 Table and chairs

3 Broad-leaved *Hosta sieboldiana*

4 Virginia creeper

5 Marguerites in tubs

6 Rose in tub

7 Brick paving

8 Shade-loving ferns

9 Hogweed

The seating area is flanked by a wall clad with ivy and Virginia creeper (4). Plain brick paving creates a neutral background for gray-leaved shrubby marguerites (*Chrysanthemum frutescens*) (5). An unusual feature is the oleander (*Nerium*) with its tall pale stem. This produces lovely white or pink flowers. In temperate gardens it would thrive under glass. The bark is poisonous.

Left **The giant hogweed** (*Heracleum Mantegazzianum*) (9), can tower to an overwhelming 12ft (3m). Although conventionally regarded as unsuitable for herbaceous borders, it possesses exactly the kind of architectural presence that is called for in a contemporary garden such as this. Its unkempt beauty challenges the restraint of the other plants and the refinement of the rest of the garden design. At its base, the mound of dahlia-like leaves belongs to *Bidens*, which produces yellow flowers in late summer. An alternative choice for a similar effect would be *Coreopsis*.
● Another herbaceous perennial that might be used as a striking vertical feature is *Crambe cordifolia*.

Above **A border** of shade-loving plants, including ferns and *Hosta sieboldiana*, lines the north-facing wall. Pot plants carry the foliage out onto the terrace, giving an impression of rampant growth. *Miscanthus* overhangs from the neighboring plot.

A WINDOW FOR SHELTER

It may seem paradoxical for a garden to have a "window". However, in this patio garden a sheet of frosted glass (shown in the plan and in the photograph on the opposite page, bottom left) serves to provide shelter from wind without creating conditions of shade. As a bonus, the bobbled pattern of the glass also obscures the view of unattractive modern houses nearby. The result is a pleasingly simple, sunny terrace.

The planting is rich and varied. The permanent, architectural nature of a good selection of evergreens provides an attractive contrast with the wide variety of deciduous leaf shapes. Bright flowers in spring and summer freckle the scene with color—in particular, pinks, reds and whites. Behind the seat is a mass of impatience.

The profusion of plants, spilling freely over the margins of the space, contrasts appealingly with the square grid of the paving. Such contrasts of the formal and the random—or *apparently* random—are the basis of many excellent designs.

The illustration (right) shows the garden in spring, with tulips and other spring-flowering annuals. The photographs show summer color. This versatility, obtained by generous use of pot plants, is one of the strengths of this delightful garden.

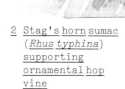

1   Bulbs for spring color, impatience for summer color

2   Stag's horn sumac (*Rhus typhina*) supporting ornamental hop vine

3   Grid-like pattern of paving stones

4   Partition of bobbled glass

5   Container plants for versatility of flower color

6   Bench

7   Tulips

8   Grapevine on trellis attached to house wall

Above left **A grapevine**, supported by trelliswork on the house wall, towers over *Ceanothus* and a mass of pansies.
● Although rather a late-season starter, the grapevine (*Vitis vinifera*) has a prodigious capacity for growth and an ability to blot out brickwork with its acid green foliage once the summer is under way.

Left **A stag's horn sumac** makes a fine support for an ornamental hop and forms the centerpiece of an elaborate composition of foliage and flowers anchored by variegated ivy. A tender jasmine, just visible in front of the glass partition, provides pretty broken foliage and beautifully fragrant flowers in summer.

Above **The pale-toned paving slabs** are left uncluttered in the central area–the pot plants are limited to the margins. This uninterrupted paving, however limited in extent, increases the feeling of spaciousness.

AN EXOTIC MINIATURE

This treatment of a tiny triangular yard with brick walls and a concrete base, proves that there are no hard and fast rules about planning a small garden. An agreeable leafy corner can be created in the most improbable places.

Since ripping out concrete and replacing it with soil is usually a major task, the solution, as shown here, is to grow plants in abundance in troughs, planters and pots, imaginatively re-using any available wooden boxes, bricks or old tables, that would otherwise be thrown away, to support them. This approach provides flowers and foliage at several levels.

Although gardens made in this random, accumulative way might appear, at first glance, simple to manage, they do in fact require plenty of maintenance. The pot plants need constant watering in hot, dry weather – usually the biggest commitment and chore. The compost for growing plants in pots should ideally contain a high proportion of peat moss, and this tends to dry out quickly. To provide good growing conditions, you need to keep the peat moss constantly moist.

One way to maintain the moisture level is to stand the pots on a layer of fine gravel, which should be kept waterlogged. An alternative option is to buy irrigation equipment which will enable any number of pots to be watered at the turn of a faucet from drippers set on the compost surface. For very busy people, a humidity-controlled automatic valve can even be installed to dispense with the chore of having to turn on the faucet. If irrigation equipment is being used, it is important to conceal the scramble of plastic pipes, so as not to spoil the overall appearance of the garden.

1 Small mirror hung on wall

2 Scallop shells used as attractive natural planters

3 Planting boxes on wall provide extra seclusion

4 Tea-trolley used to support pot plants, lifting them toward light

5 Old coffee table creates extra planting level

6 Entrance

Right **Broad-leaved Fatsia japonica** can bring an exotic, jungly look to a small yard. Next to it, on the recycled table (5), are a tumble of trailing lobelia and a potted *Neoregelia marechalii*. In such a cloistered situation, you might wish to add color by a careful choice of shade-loving plants, such as begonias, astilbes and *Mimulus*. Another way to enrich the planting would be to introduce non-hardy pot plants in the summer.

Below **When space is at a premium**, hanging baskets come into their own. Also, the character of a small yard can be improved by whitewashing the brick walls. In a damp warm climate, a covering of moss will make the walls appear less brash. An unusual feature here is the vase with dead branches forming an abstract sculpture. Trailing lobelia and *Campanula isophylla* introduce harmonizing colors.

Above **Window boxes** placed on top of an existing wall pleasantly heighten the barrier between neighbors. Trailing lobelias, planted along their edges, soon banish the plainness of the wooden sides.

● Tradescantias, including the variegated version above the mirror, are surprisingly hardy and will survive many winters outdoors, adding variety to trailing foliage.

● A mirror like this one, mounted on a wall, is too small to make a garden appear more extensive, but will create attractive highlights when the sun catches it.

● A conch shell with a plant grown in it is an unusual way to liven up a small area. Such improvised containers should have a hole drilled through the base, to permit adequate drainage.

BEYOND THE PATIO DOOR

This tiny courtyard garden—only 16ft × 20ft (5m × 6m)—was designed to be viewed through a large, glazed patio door. For continuity's sake, a similar ground surface treatment was used both for the garden and for the adjacent room. Outdoors the paving is offset with areas of round sea-washed pebbles in the planting area—an effective and natural way to introduce variety.

The conventional fence, made of unstained timber panels, has been enlivened by trellis raised above it at the far end, and set into the panels along one side. In screening and enclosing the garden, the trellis thus adds to the sense of the area as a direct extension of the house itself. Trellis, adorned with flowers and climbing foliage, laid against other parts of the fence, compensates for the lack of planting space on the ground. The opportunities for vertical gardening have been further exploited in the placing of two timber upright frames, festooned with plants, on either side of the patio doors.

The view from the house has been taken thoroughly into account: the sculptural figure, for example, can be seen from the main indoor seating area, while the greenery near the doors seems to strain to cross the threshold into the house itself.

1 Trellis attached to fence to increase seclusion

2 Statue with broad-leaved hostas at base

3 More profuse planting, including prolific foxgloves, bounds the pool

4 Uncluttered pool with single clump of iris and a lily

5 Climbing roses

6 Two unplanted garden pots

7 Closely-packed pebbles break monotony of paving

8 Patio doors

Left **The raised pool** introduces a change in contour, emphasized by using the same gray paving slabs for the pool surround as for the ground-level treatment. In the foreground is *Rheum palmatum*.
● A raised feature such as this pool, which could just as easily have been a raised bed or a well, creates a perimeter track around the garden. Even in the smallest plot, it is always a good idea to create a distinct route for exploration.

Above **Foliage** of bamboo, fern and wisteria makes a splendid foil for a beautiful pot.
● Sometimes it is worth resisting the temptation to fill every pot with plants. If well-designed, an empty pot can look just as striking.

121

REFLECTIONS OF SPAIN

There is a distinctly Spanish flavor in this tiny patio garden. In Cordoba, near the southern tip of Spain, you can glimpse gardens like this through wrought-iron gateways as you wander the narrow streets.

Creating such a garden in a tiny basement courtyard is an art in itself. Before choosing your plants, you must carefully work out how much sunlight the space will receive. Even in midsummer the sun may penetrate only briefly, which means that you would be restricted to shade-tolerant plants. However, many basement areas, as well as being sheltered from wind, also receive direct sunlight for part of the day, enabling you to grow sun-loving plants of great character such as the fuchsia here.

A large mirror on one of the walls of the patio amplifies available light, reflecting it into shady corners—as do the white-painted walls and, to some extent, the light-colored paving. The mirror also helps to make the garden feel more spacious. If mirrors are used effectively, a single plant in a pot can be made to appear like a jungly thicket.

1 Brick-retained raised bed in two tiers

2 Brick-retained bed with hydrangea and other bold plants

3 Clematis trained to climb round and frame mirror

4 Fuchsia provides bright, long-lasting color

5 Statues

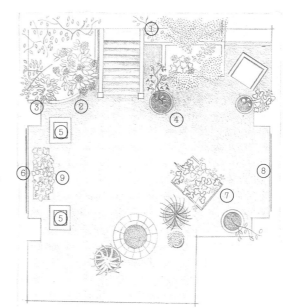

6 Large mirror reflects light and creates feeling of spaciousness

7 Wheelbarrow containing pelargoniums

8 Doors to house

9 Stone planter containing classic summer bedding annuals

Left **Two tiers of beds** retained by brick hold pelargoniums, white petunias and blue trailing lobelias, with variegated *Euonymus* at the back. Reinforcing the newel post of the steps, a blood-red fuchsia (4) catches the eye. A grapevine, *Vitis vinifera* 'Brandt', clambers up toward the light along the underside of the steps. This photograph was taken in summer: in spring, flower color is supplied by the jasmine and *Ceanothus* on the trellis.

Above **Fuchsias**, ivy-leaved pelargoniums, white hollyhocks and lobelias combine here in a planting which has all the artistry of a flower arrangement.
● Container gardening offers lots of scope in a patio basement such as this. Even water lilies make good container plants, and tiny specimens such as *Nymphaea tetragona* will flourish in a foot of water in a terracotta bowl.

Right **Surmounting the mirror** is a pierced screen supporting a *Clematis Jackmanii*, whose abundant large purple flowers are set off by the large white heads of the hydrangea in the brick planter. The mirror doubles the effect of impatience, petunias and elegant statuary immediately in front of it, as well as reflecting a wheel-barrow full of pelargoniums farther away.

JAPANESE SIMPLICITY

A long session with clippers and pruning shears several times a year, regular mowing of the lawn and minimal weeding are all it takes to keep this garden looking attractive. Setting a permanent scene with low-maintenance evergreen plants, the garden reflects a distinctly Japanese style that also finds favor in America.

Gardens like this run the risk of seeming static. Certainly, there is little of the excitement of gardens designed to change dramatically with the seasons. However, if planned with sufficient conviction and style, as in this case, the effect can be pleasing throughout the year. Success depends on exploiting the full potential of each tree and shrub to reveal unusual sculptural forms. Singling out particular trees and shaving them into striking shapes meant to suggest rocks, or

perhaps distant hills, is a typical feature of Japanese gardening. The simple planting here simulates the pine-clad rocks of Japan's Inland Sea—the original inspiration of the country's gardening style.

When planning an evergreen garden of this kind, it is important to compensate for the limited color scheme by providing contrasts of foliage texture and a wide range of different shades of green.

Above **A bizarre column** alongside the door of the house is created by a cypress tree (*Chamaecyparis*) subjected to the art of topiary (6). Alongside is a gourd (*Cucurbita*).

1 Closely mown lawn

2 Japanese-style paving stones surrounded by gravel

3 Island bed containing clipped Japanese maple, pine tree and azaleas

4 Clipped cypress forms dramatic sculptural feature (see page 126)

5 Micro apple tree in simple bowl (see page 127)

6 Clipped cypress next to door of house

Left **Pine tree boughs**
have been stripped bare
in places so that the
remaining foliage
appears like clouds
floating past mast-like
trunks (3). In contrast,
next to the pine, the
naturally spreading
crown of the Japanese
maple (shown here in
fruit, in late summer)
has been shorn to a
smooth dome. When in
bloom in late spring,
the deciduous azaleas at
the foot of the pine
change the mood of this
distinctive island bed
with a blaze of color.
Beneath the umbrella of
the maple is a mass of
begonias.

● The bedding begonia,
B. semperflorens, is
unusual among annuals
in its tolerance for the
shade under trees. It
provides a 2-month
display of flowers.

Chamaecyparis pisifera, a small-leaved cypress, can fill all kinds of roles–from providing tall barriers to making playful patterns like those displayed here (4).

● Boxwood is one of the most popular evergreens for clipping and hedging. Other evergreens that are suitable for clipping closely are yew or holly.

Yew is ideal for large shapes: for sculptural forms on a smaller scale it would be preferable to use box. Many botanical gardens have specimen plots where

different kinds of hedges can be compared.

Left **Stones**, small tree-stumps and spears of giant horsetail (*Equisetum*) on a bed of gravel create the type of simple but enigmatic composition that is typical of Japanese gardening. The effect depends partly on the dramatic contrast of scale, and the slenderness of the planting juxtaposed with the massive rock.

 Above **An apple tree** (5) has been dwarfed to bonsai proportions by restricting its roots in an earthenware pot attractively mounted on a stool-like frame. The large rock and the mat-forming plant turn this composition into a miniature landscape.
● As an alternative to bonsai, you could buy a miniature fruit tree, up to 3ft (1 meter) high. The fruit will be normal-sized.

PURE THEATER

With thorough planning and a tasteful choice of plants and materials, you can create an impression of luxury, as in this garden designed to produce a stage-like effect. Nearly all the plants have been given a solo position to emphasize their distinctive textures. The brickwork, random paving and ironwork are all of high quality, their location deliberate and purposeful, to achieve maximum theatrical impact.

The terrace area is sufficiently generous to allow plenty of room for relaxing, without being disproportionately large compared with the rest of the garden. Its shape, too, is simple but interesting, with a half-moon extension, like a bay window. Its surface is relieved by potted architectural plants, such as the strategically placed agave and hostas.

The random paving is splendidly laid, using stone fragments with bold, positive shapes to form intriguing patterns. The golden rule is to be generous with the cement grouting, emphasizing the individuality of each fragment. This rule should also be adhered to when laying hand-made, rectangular paving slabs, which always vary in size.

There is enough soothing green lawn to lie on and to act as a background for the play of sunlight, casting shadows through surrounding trees. The lawn is well framed by foliage. The planting contains a good mixture of trees, shrubs and annual and perennial herbaceous plants of varying shapes and sizes, ensuring interest throughout the year.

Gateways that allow a glimpse of vegetation beyond the boundary can make any garden appear more extensive. Here, the gate is an integral feature of the overall design. Another ploy is the placing of matching decorative objects in different parts of the garden. The rustic vase on top of this gateway complements that on the terrace wall—a subtle way of drawing the whole design together.

Gardens as carefully contrived as this one tend to look too perfect initially, but improve with time as materials weather and the plants mature and become less disciplined. A few natural flaws in a garden are always an asset.

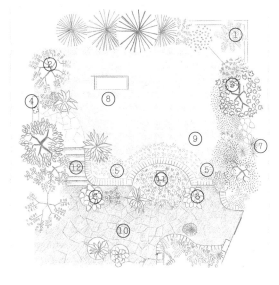

Right **"Elephant ear"** leaves of the *Paulownia tomentosa* tree in the background and the grapevine *Vitis coignetiae* on the trelliswork contrast well with the bright little spear heads of the goldheart ivy nearby and the spiky swords of the agave (bottom right), hostas (*H. sieboldiana*) and spiky *Cordyline terminalis* in the foreground. The semi-circular brick wall, topped with a mauve ring of the annual *Ageratum houstonianum*, makes a fine setting for a delicate classical statue.

Above **A brick "book end"** corner feature is a masterstroke in any small garden. This one is relieved of heaviness by its turreted top. Creating a sheltered spot, it incorporates an alcove to house a bust, exquisite high-relief tiles and a corpulent fern in an attractive tall pot. It elegantly terminates the view across the garden and masks any eyesores beyond.

Right **A made-to-measure gate** in cast iron is well worth the considerable expense. This one has an attractive spiderweb design. The ivy and Virginia creeper are rapidly concealing the newness of this feature. A bold agave, at ground level, sets off the climbers splendidly. (In cold climates, a yucca could be used instead.)

A CONTROLLED WILDERNESS

It is hard to believe that this garden is sited near the center of Washington D.C. Any urban feeling has been obliterated by the sheer profusion of vegetation, in which the massive clump of ornamental *Miscanthus* grass–big enough to conceal a tiger–has been allowed to dominate. In contrast to the sword-like leaves of the ornamental grasses, there is a sprinkling of showy, colorful plants, such as tulips (see page 133) and spring-flowering bergenias.

In a deliberately-created wilderness such as this, flowering plants stationed deep in the garden need the robustness and stature of, for example, the yellow, black-eyed susans (shown in the photograph below), to make any impact at all when viewed from the house.

Looking from the terrace, the garden jealously preserves its secrets: there is nothing to hint at its length, and only one of the boundaries is visible–a rustic timber fence set on a low brick wall. The dark shadows cast by the trees at the end of the garden add to the sense of mystery. Beneath the dense foliage, conditions are ideal for shade-loving plants, such as ferns, to prosper.

Making a wild-looking garden like this is a good way to deal with any long, narrow plot.

Perennial black-eyed susans (*Rudbeckia*) (3) are best used in massed planting. ● Today, some excellent compact varieties of *Rudbeckia* are available for the smaller garden. Lasting well in water, they make good cutting flowers. The flowering season is late summer and early autumn.

1 <u>Tulips</u> and <u>forget-me-nots</u>

2 <u>Stepping stones</u>

3 <u>Black-eyed susans</u> (*Rudbeckia*) <u>add splash of yellow</u>

4 *Miscanthus* <u>grass</u>

5 <u>Hollyhocks</u>

6 <u>Clematis</u>

7 <u>Timber fence on brick wall base</u>

8 <u>Steps up from house</u>

9 <u>Japanese snowbell tree</u> (*Styrax japonica*)

10 <u>Sunken terrace area</u>

A wealth of bold foliage textures near the house adds to the impression of exotic luxuriance.

Groundcover in the brick-retained bed is provided by the broad, fleshy leaves of spring-flowering bergenias, eulalia (*Miscanthus sinensis*) (4) and lilyturf (*Liriope*). The red flower is hibiscus.

● Rising from the grasses is a Japanese snowbell tree (*Styrax japonica*) (9)—a small, loose-branched tree which bears pendulous white flowers in early summer.

Below **Blurring** the right-hand boundary of the Washington D.C. garden described on the previous pages are *Clematis* 'Mellie Moser' (6) and the tall *Miscanthus* grass (4).
● Small urns like this can be filled with summer color, and shifted about at will to change the picture.

Right **Stone slabs** (2), irregularly set to form a meandering path through the garden, allow access in wet weather. They also make an excellent foil to the patches of lawn, making the ground treatment more interesting. The introduction of large pots creates a welcome change in planting level.

Above **Massing tulips** (I) is a wonderful way to provide a spring color spectacular. Here, two types of large-flowered Darwin tulips are mixed with yellow lily-flowered hybrids, with a foreground of forget-me-knots.
● The disadvantage of bulbs is that they do not leave much room, in a garden of limited space, for perennial plants to take on their role when the bulbs have finished flowering. Of course, you can rear interesting, later-season plants elsewhere in the garden. But if you have time for an intensive-management approach to gardening, you may prefer instead to plant annuals to take the place of the bulbs, as soon as the bulbs have died back.

A WEALTH OF DETAIL

This is an enthusiast's garden, combining lawn, water, paving and dwarf conifers with a wealth of floral interest—climbers, rock plants, container plants, border perennials and a sprinkling of annuals and biennials. The profusion of eye-catching detail, and the division of the space into distinct compartments, make the area seem surprisingly spacious, yet the plot is only 100ft (30m) long.

Linking the ponds is a line of standard paving slabs, gently curving towards the clematis-clad archway. A more meandering path would have produced a less formal effect, but this arrangement has the advantage of leading the eye directly to the archway, with its tantalizing glimpse of fountain and sculpture. This gives an impression of distance.

A notable feature is the use of narrow passageways—for example, where the two semi-circular raised beds bulge toward each other. Such constructions help to guide movement through the garden, and create an interesting rhythm with the more open spaces of lawns and paving.

1 Secret garden with statue

2 Pools

3 Rockery

4 Garden seat (not visible from house)

5 Movable urn adds interest to lawn

6 Enclosing wall hidden by shrubs

7 Paving slabs set into lawn

8 Paved area next to house

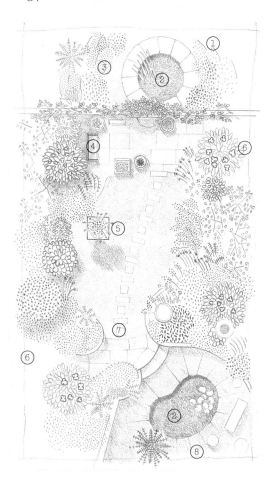

A lily pond provides a point of interest in the seating area next to the house.
● The bench beside the pool is of reconstituted stone. Such weighty sculptural forms need strong background planting so that they do not shout for attention.
● A small pond like this cannot contain both water lilies and a fountain: water lilies should always be planted in deep, still water. In winter when the leaves have shrunk, the pond will retain interest as a dark mirror.

Right **An archway** festooned in purple *Clematis Jackmanii* and white *C. Jackmanii* 'Superba' makes an enticing entrance to a garden within a garden. This one is of wrought-iron with a graceful spiral design. Beyond, an ornamental figure smaller than lifesize makes this part of the garden seem larger than it is.
● Asymmetrically-arranged containers are good for marking the entrance to a special area, such as this secret garden. Plain pots will not suffice for this important role: you must choose something more unusual.

Above **A damp, shady spot** near the pond shows a subtle use of different shades of green. The variegated *Pieris* contrasts with a carpet of pennyroyal (*Mentha pulegium*), used here in its green and golden forms. Completing the effect are an overarching fern and a clump of *Spiraea*.

Right **Stone troughs,** imaginatively planted, mark the transition from paving to lawn. The main feature plant, *Cryptomeria japonica* 'Vilmoriniana', creates a soft mound, contrasting on either side with various mossy and encrusted saxifrages. The pale pink flowers behind are toadflax (*Cymbalaria muralis*), harmonizing with the deeper pink of *Dianthus caryophyllus*. A dwarf juniper provides a vertical accent.

A VISION OF THE PAST

Grandeur is not always hungry for space. This highly-successful reinterpretation of the grand manner of a 17th-century formal garden shows how a monumental effect can sometimes be accommodated within a relatively small patch of land.

Although designed to give an effect of masonry, the heavily rusticated gateway, the pair of obelisks opposite, the arch framing the grotto, and the four pillars along the open side of the garden are actually made from weather-resistant marine plywood which has been stained an attractive dark green.

Simple trelliswork has been used as it was in the 17th century to make space dividers, which break up the garden into a series of alleys or compartments. Yew bushes planted inside the trelliswork frames will eventually fill them to make substantial hedges. The ground surface is mostly gravel, but with four small patches of lawn.

The plan is based on two central axes crossing at a square pond. Whichever way you enter the garden, there is a vista across the pond towards an eyecatching feature on the other side. Entering through the gateway, you are confronted with a mirror-like panel above a large planting container. Coming in along the other axis, between the middle pair of pillars, the view is of a rocky grotto in the Renaissance style.

The planting is minimal. Two little borders with a low box edging provide a suitable showcase for white tulips and forget-me-nots. There are two other borders with solid *Alchemilla mollis* and four with solid rue. Small balls and pyramids of box provide ornamental interest.

This would be an intriguing low-maintenance garden for a town-dweller with classical inclinations. Although it is a place for strolling and admiring rather than lounging, there are two benches positioned to give views down the whole length of the garden.

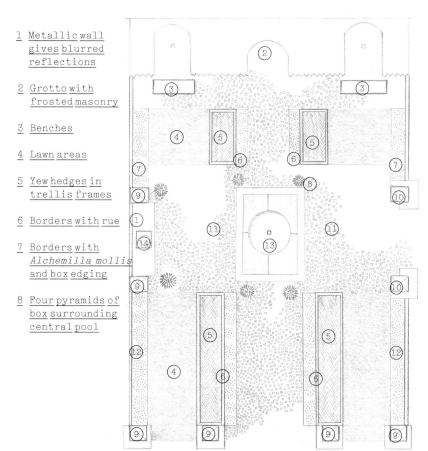

1 Metallic wall gives blurred reflections

2 Grotto with frosted masonry

3 Benches

4 Lawn areas

5 Yew hedges in trellis frames

6 Borders with rue

7 Borders with *Alchemilla mollis* and box edging

8 Four pyramids of box surrounding central pool

9 Stained timber pillars

10 Stained timber archway with broken pediment

11 Gravel areas

12 Borders with tulips and forget-me-nots, edged with box

13 Pond with central ball on a pole

14 Box ball

A grotto in the Renaissance style (2), surrounded by imitation frosted masonry, provides a backdrop for a mirrored ball and a single pot plant at ground level. The pool has an ingenious device: turning the ball revolves a plate set below water level, which in turn changes the pattern of reflections.

A mirrored ball, silvered on the inside, is the focal point of this carefully-contrived formal vista between pyramids of box, seen through an archway with rusticated piers and a broken pediment. Beneath the ball is a classical-style planting case of box and *Festuca glauca*. The shiny metallic surface behind catches subdued reflections. In the center of the pond, the ball on a pole gives height in the same way as a fountain does, but without a costly installation. The fabric sheets attached to the trellis work in the foreground serve as temporary screening devices.

● Arranging a garden on two crossed axes, with judicious use of trelliswork, hedges or other screening features, is an excellent way to give the illusion of greater space. Looking through the arch, we see the alleys leading off at either side, but cannot judge their length and are thus at liberty to imagine them stretching farther than they do.

ANCHORED BY AN OCTAGON

One solution to the challenge of a long thin plot is to divide the garden into two segments of lawn separated by an area of formal planting. Here, the division is created by an octagonal area of concentric beds and paving. In a central area of this kind, the geometrical pattern could be marked out in a variety of planting schemes—for example, sculpted box hedges with a rose garden in the center. In this case a young lavender hedge is beginning to establish itself around the outer octagon, with white *Nicotiana alata* given pride of place. Two yellow mounds of *Alchemilla mollis* add sculptural form. Another approach altogether in this central area would be to make a maze of turf or low-growing box.

Strips of paving on either side of the first lawn link the octagon with a stone terrace adjacent to the house. The tall, thick hedge around the boundary incorporates many existing shrubs, such as a fine camellia at the far end (a privilege of mild-climate gardens), a *Weigela* and two silver-leaved weeping pears. A weeping willow in the next-door garden droops over into this one, blotting out the view beyond.

1 Lawn areas

2 Paved terrace in front of house

3 Bench flanked by planting boxes (see page 140)

4 Weeping pear trees (*Pyrus salicifolia* 'Pendula')

5 Camellia

6 *Nicotiana alata*

7 Octagonal bed containing lavender

8 Yellow *Alchemilla mollis*

9 Smooth paving

10 Climbing roses

11 Clematis

Right In the octagon area (shown here before the plants are established) the temptation to include a central eye-catcher such as a sundial or statue has been resisted. Instead, the impact relies on foliage, flowers and high-quality paving. A giant mullein (*Verbascum*), stationed on the paving, alleviates its flatness. The dark-leafed camellia at the end of the garden will produce large, showy blooms in spring.
● Instead of an area of flowers, an octagonal pool could be used to separate two areas of lawn.

Above **A pink rambling rose** adds color to the thickly planted boundary.
● Rambling roses are distinct from climbers in having long, pliable stems (rather than stiff ones) carrying trusses of small flowers in the summer. Unlike climbers, ramblers are not repeat-flowering. They can be encouraged to climb if given a suitable support.

Growth is usually vigorous.

A bench (3), framed by square planting boxes, is overhung by branches of a weeping pear (*Pyrus salicifolia* 'Pendula'), whose leaves are covered with silvery hairs until early summer.

Left **Tress-like catkins** of *Garrya elliptica*, combined with its dark-green foliage, make a marvellously rich background for a display of white single-flowered clematis.
● Large-flowered clematis hybrids will flower in early summer and again in late summer—unless you have pruned hard to control growth, in which case they will flower only once.

Above **Irises** always make an eye-catching feature. Even when the flowers have faded, the leaves will provide a bright background for the rich purple of nearby pansies—which will bloom for a long season.

DIAGONALS FOR MOVEMENT

There is a distinct Japanese influence in this garden, apparent in the combination of evergreens, gravel, timber, plants displayed in solo positions, and stone artifacts such as the lantern illustrated on this page (below right). But although this design embraces the good taste and subtlety of the best oriental styles, it is also thoroughly attuned to the Western temperament.

What first strikes the eye is the strong visual framework—a pattern of two diagonal wooden plank walkways, arranged at right angles to sets of stout wooden beams sunk into a panel of gravel. This makes the garden resemble a giant, low-level, geometric sculpture. The plot would be interesting even if there were no planting at all. Diagonals used in this way always introduce a sense of movement into a garden. In another situation, a similar effect could be achieved with brick pathways arranged diagonally.

The evergreens that surround the central space, giving ample seclusion, have been chosen for their rich variety of textures and different shades of green, with subtle brushstrokes of blue. Ferns and other shade-loving plants are used beneath the evergreen canopy. Rhododendrons provide seasonal color but are not used too prominently, as they tend to look bleak in winter.

1 Garden shed obscured by greenery

2 Mixed planting, predominantly evergreen, masks boundary

3 Steps up to raised lawn

4 Walkways consisting of timber planks

5 Gravel of different grades separated by thin wooden slats

6 Prickly pear

7 Cotoneaster for ground cover

8 Rocks retaining bed

Above **The austere simplicity** of the timber planks serves as a foil for rich planting that is full of contrasts—for example, the bold, strap-like leaves of yucca stationed alongside the column-like habit of a cypress. The ground-cover plant *Cotoneaster dammeri* (7) has been used to fill the right-angle between the walkway and the wooden slats.

Above **A small stone lantern** in the Japanese style makes an eyecatching feature among the mixed evergreens. Rhododendrons at either side are offset by sharp pine needles and the large-leaved *Rodgersia tabularis*, which bears plumes of white summer flowers. ● The rhododendron here—*R. yakusimamum*—is notably compact and free-flowering. Deep pink buds mature to pale pink and then white.

Mysterious shadows cast by the evergreens effectively mask the garden's boundary. Despite its wealth of tones and textures, the foliage might have seemed too heavy and static without the relief provided by the diagonal timbers (4), which add a sense of movement to the whole garden. Notable among the plants is the mature cypress which dominates the upper area of this picture.

● Gravel is the least expensive material for a hard surface–both to buy and lay. Unembellished, it has little charm or interest, but it makes an excellent basis for dramatic contrasts, especially with timber edgings.

● Alternative edgings for gravel panels of this type might include a two-foot border of brickwork or stone, or a strip of moss or large pebbles.

● It is effective to juxtapose different colors or grades of gravel, provided that they are separated by distinct partitions, as here.

Above **Winter aconites** (*Eranthis hyemalis*), whose yellow cup-shaped flowers appear in late winter, are sited in a slightly raised peaty bed, enclosed by moss-clad rocks of volcanic lava. These plants thrive in such shady spots, beneath trees and shrubs.

Right **Magnolias** have the most splendid flowers of any trees—that is, looked at individually rather than *en masse*. The showiest are those of *M.* x *Soulangiana*, shown here, which flowers before the leaves emerge. The tree has an air of distinction all year round, whether in bare structure or in leaf.
● Magnolias require fertile soil, preferably acid, and a spot in sun or partial shade.
● Where space is restricted, a good choice is *M. stellata*, which grows to only 4–5ft (1–1.5m). It bears scented, creamy-white flowers in spring.

Above **A prickly pear** (*Opuntia*) (6) in proud isolation displays its sculptural form—like some brash polyp from another world. Note the juxtaposition of different grades of gravel either side of the wooden slats.
● This cactus is surprisingly hardy—some varieties can live outdoors as far north as Massachusetts.

Above **A wall sculpture** in metal, representing fruiting bodies of the wood rot against which this fence has been treated, is yet another highly individual feature of this garden. Fronds of weeping blue cedar (*Cedrus atlantica* 'Glauca Pendula') serves as an effective frame, contrasting with a mound of box.

● Most cedars grow too large for a modest garden, but there are compact and weeping varieties that will stay within bounds.

A COTTAGE WITH A DIFFERENCE

A cottage of strong rural character imposes its own disciplines on the garden designer. Rigid elements can co-exist with this kind of architecture, but they should be mingled with informality. However, there is no need for cottage gardens to become stereotypes. This is a good example of a garden that is pretty without falling into the trap of the picture-postcard cliché.

The plot is much less densely-planted than the usual English cottage style would dictate. However, because the plants are bold, the area seems richly clad. A prominent feature has been made of the ground surface: timber decking is juxtaposed in one corner of the garden with more traditional paving slabs. The decking has enabled the designer to create a flat veranda-style garden (though with distinct steps that add interest to the surface) on a sloping site.

A jacuzzi is placed on its own slightly raised platform and screened for privacy. Notice how the boundary of the main decking uses a mature tree as a corner post.

Although remarkably unconventional, this is above all a place for relaxation and enjoyment.

1 Wooden decking

2 Jacuzzi and pot plants beneath pergola (see page 149)

3 Boulders

4 Pine tree used as "corner post", with shelf for pot plants (see page 148)

5 Paved area

6 Front door of cottage

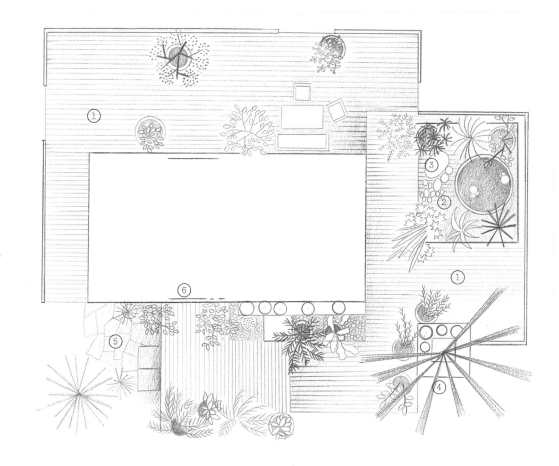

The path to the front door begins as paving stones and then mounts to timber decking. A Virginia creeper and pot-grown ivy fulfil the traditional role of roses around the cottage door. A clump of ornamental grass (*Miscanthus sacchariflorus*) stands tall in the foreground, with *Alchemilla mollis* at its foot. Arching into this view from the left is a Turkish hazel (*Corylus colurna*), which produces long yellow catkins in late winter.

● Overlapped paving stones, as used here in the foreground, are a good way to deal with a slight gradient.

147

Left **A catalpa tree** and various other plants in pots can easily be moved around the deck to vary the scene and alter the pattern of light and shade. These plants are well combined with climbers, such as the elephant-eared grapevine (*Vitis coignetiae*) on the pergola. From this viewpoint the jacuzzi is hidden by a screen of bamboo.

● You need to think carefully about the planting before laying a timber deck. It may be advisable to leave holes here and there for deep-rooted climbers that cannot be grown in pots.

Above **A pine tree bole** like this makes a perfect place to cluster pots of plants (4). Tree trunks can easily be fitted with shelves to provide extra planting space above ground level. Terracotta pots convey a traditional feel appropriate to the cottage architecture.

Right **A still life** of boulders and pebbles conjures up seaside associations appropriate to the foaming water of a jacuzzi (2). The largest boulder has been incised with a spiral pattern for extra interest. An impression of dense greenery is created by the *Phormium tenax*, *Fatsia japonica*, coconut palm and, at the left of the picture, *Ligularia* 'Rocket' and *Cyperus* sedge.

THE CLARITY OF BLACK AND WHITE

Planting is concentrated around the margins of this small roof garden with its distinctive tiled paving pattern. This is a good solution if the roof itself is not strong enough to take a heavy load. Here, planted urns tower against the background of trees, their considerable weight taken by substantial peripheral walls whose corners they announce with a flourish. Flower colour is contained in unusual window boxes ingeniously set into the parapet. The containers that are scattered around the seating area are mostly lightweight to avoid overloading.

The surface of a roof garden can often be dull, but here the black and white checkerboard pattern of lightweight tiles creates a striking effect.

Surrounded by a rich tangle of trees, this garden needs very little planting or ornament to turn it into a magical space.

Left **A potentilla** (*P. fruticosa*) (2) forms mounds of yellow flowers which last through the summer. Red and yellow wallflowers (*Cheiranthus*) in the window boxes, pelargoniums and pink begonias add to the colorful picture.

● *Potentilla fruticosa* is a good choice for a roof garden, as it is hardy and thrives in plenty of light, preferring full sun and well-drained soil. The shade of yellow varies widely, from lemon to gold. It is thus advisable to buy the plant when it is in flower.

Below **A treadle table** for a sewing machine has been converted to make an ideal marble-topped table. This is a good example of improvising to add individual style. A simple potted begonia completes the effect.

1 Bird feeder

2 *Potentilla* in wooden tub

3 Urns mark corners of parapet wall

4 Window troughs built into parapet

5 Hardy annuals in plastic and terracotta pots near perimeter

6 Lightweight black and white tiles make a bold pattern

7 Table improvised from sewing machine stand

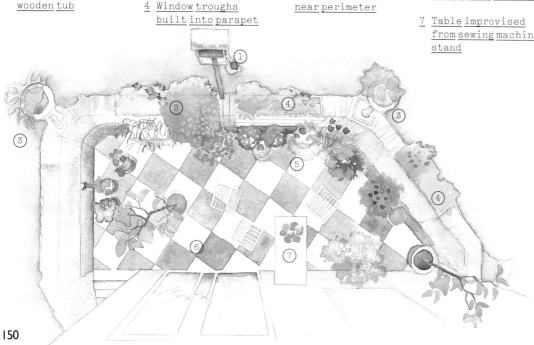

This bird feeder (1) is well sited to attract birds from neighboring treetops, and also makes an attractive sculptural object in its own right.

● Birds can be a mixed blessing in a garden—especially a paved area which is likely to accumulate deposits. They may also plunder precious berries and fruits. In some town gardens, remember that a large bird feeder may encourage undesirable pigeons. Small-scale fruit trees may be covered with nets to prevent them from being plundered.

A LOUVERED BALCONY

Even a small balcony can support plenty of attractive plants if full use is made of hanging baskets, as in this louvered high-level jacuzzi garden.

The slatted panels serve as a windbreak and provide shade in a striped pattern, while allowing plenty of air to circulate and light to enter. The open side looks away from the prevailing wind, offering a view over treetops. Care has been taken to create an interesting pattern in the woodwork, with verticals, diagonals and horizontals producing a sense of liveliness. This is reinforced by the bubbling water of the jacuzzi, whose functional purpose is softened by a margin of spider plants and other potted greenery, giving it a more natural appearance.

The benches along the side of the house are supplemented by chairs around a circular table which echoes the size and shape of the tub.

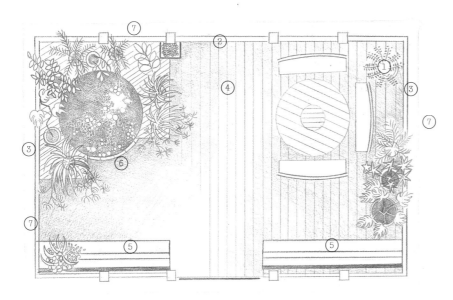

1 Hanging baskets make optimum use of space

2 Open view onto trees beyond

3 Diagonal slatted surround with pot plants and more hanging baskets

4 Timber deck matches sides

5 Integral benches

6 Fitted jacuzzi

7 Louvers screen sun and wind

A hanging basket (1) often works well with two ingredients—one vertical and one trailing—to make use of space above and below. Here the feathery foliage of ornamental asparagus (*A. Sprengeri*) is balanced by twining, dark-green, leathery leaves of *Trachelospermum jasminoides*.
● Open-mesh baskets lined with sphagnum moss tend to blend in with their background more than solid containers.

A lush surround of ferns, philodendrons, rubber plants and trailing spider plants around the jacuzzi combines with the filtered sunlight to convey a tropical mood. Overhanging the jacuzzi surround is a pair of spider plants (*Chlorophytum elatum*). The *Monstera deliciosa* and rubber plant (*Ficus elastica*) add height to the arrangement. A jacuzzi will create its own microclimate, which you must bear in mind when choosing adjacent plants.

WALKING ON GLASS

This secluded roof area has been turned into an elegant outdoor sitting room with a French or Italian feel. An adjacent medieval church with its happily placed lantern lends a detail of its historic facade, shown in the photograph opposite. Transparent panels set into the timber-covered roof let light into the room below, without impinging upon the space available. Indeed, they have become a design element in themselves, preventing the roof surface from being too monotonous.

Privet bushes trimmed to hemispheres are a major feature of the planting, supplemented by box in pyramid form. Although box is often used in formal arrangements, here the grouping is casual. A timber bench around two sides of the roof is used not only for seating but also as a shelf for further pot plants. Ivy at the top of the stairs makes a welcoming impression.

Creating a roof garden like this would be relatively inexpensive and quick, provided that no structural work was necessary.

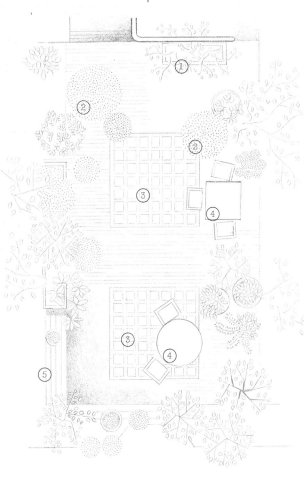

1 Ivy concealing drainpipe and adorning stairs

2 Clipped evergreens in tubs with trailing lobelias at base

3 Skylights flush with timber-covered roof

4 White garden furniture matches color of stair rails

5 Bench lining two adjacent sides of garden

The view towards the house shows a lantern by the door, specially placed here to echo the similar lantern on the church, shown in the picture opposite. The ornamental cherry (*Prunus avium* 'Plena') on the right-hand wall and a 'Canary Bird' rose on the left both flower profusely, yielding fragrant blooms at different times of year. At the extreme left of this view, in the foreground, is a *Fatsia japonica*.

Wires stretched from one wall to the other support a passion flower (*Passiflora caerulea*), which in time will provide a lush green canopy. The sheltered location offers some protection for this flowering climber. In a temperate climate, its top growth may be killed by frost, but unless the winter is exceptionally harsh, new stems will rapidly arise from its base. The conical clipped box (*Buxus sempervirens*) and dome-shaped privet (*Ligustrum ovalifolium*) have been given trailing plants at their feet, with a predominance of lobelia spilling over the large pots. A ruffled ivy (*Hedera cristata*) drapes the stairwell.

● *Passiflora caerulea* bears striking blue and white flowers between early summer and early fall, followed by egg-shaped orange fruits.

COMING IN TO LAND

Building an ambitious roof garden, such as this one, often has to be left to an expert. On an established building, considerable changes will be necessary if heavy features such as ponds or raised beds are to be supported without damaging the structure below. The job is much easier if the roof garden is planned as part of the building from the beginning.

The basic design shown here could easily be modified for a ground-level garden as well.

Essentially, the plot is a square with two smaller squares inset at opposite corners – one occupied by a pool, the other by a pergola, which makes an attractive seating area. A dramatic bird sculpture in eye-catching white dominates the pool, which is edged on one side by a square raised bed whose style echoes the peripheral raised beds on three sides.

Looking from the pergola, the swan and chimney make an effective sculptural grouping.
● A minor feature placed in proximity with a major one can have a reinforcing effect. Without the more striking swan, this chimney might attract more interest than it warrants.

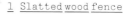

1 Slatted wood fence

2 White-flowering spirea in an easy-to-maintain area surrounding the pool

3 White swan with fountain adds movement

4 Hostas, small clump of iris and long-flowering broom in square raised bed

5 Raised beds

6 Simply paved concrete flooring

7 Pergola with trailing plants

The grass Phalaris arundinacea 'Picta', with Euonymus 'Fortunei', red-flowering broom and pink-flowering Polygonum bistorta, softens the eaves of a gable roof. This raised bed is ideal for moisture-loving plants, which benefit from the rainwater run-off.

Lush-leaved hostas, spiky iris and a broom (*Genista lydia*) flourish in spectacular contrast in the poolside raised bed. The shrubs surrounding the more inaccessible parts of the pool have been chosen mainly because they are easy to maintain. The spirea carries profuse star-like flowers on slender, arching stems. Also featured are *Hebe* (a tender shrub) (in front of the chimney) and *Cotoneaster congestus*.
● Fountains can be used to add a sense of movement to a dynamic statue or sculpture. Here, a broad spray ingeniously conjures up the bird coming in to land.

157

UNDER THE GRAPEVINE

In hot climates, a deep shady veranda can be used to create a special kind of leafy garden that gives respite from full sun while offering no barrier to refreshing breezes.

Plants such as grapevines can be trained to use the roof crossbeams as climbing frames, provided that the roof is glazed, as in this case, to admit plenty of light. Sunlight passing through the leaves will create an inviting green shade, providing ideal conditions for giant ferns and other large-leaved jungle dwellers.

If so much heavy greenery begins to feel a little oppressive, pots of brightly colored flowering plants, reared elsewhere, could be brought into the area to provide relief. Many exotics, such as camellias and bougainvilleas, will perform well under such conditions.

The broad veranda shown here is simply designed, relying for its effect on a wealth of foliage in pots. The house wall is brimming with bold, contrasting leaf forms, while on the open side a second row of planting is used to define the boundary.

Here and there, rocks and coarse gravel have been laid in small groups as visual "anchors" for the plants, and to prevent the design from seeming too transitory.

The corner post can sometimes look unsettlingly flimsy. Here, a trellis arch has been added at the far end (opposite the brick arch) to create a more substantial effect.

1 Trellis for climbing plants

2 *Alocasia*

3 Light-colored paving creates foil for greenery

4 Round table and matching benches offset the corridor-like shape of the veranda

5 Brick arch

6 Potted ferns and other shade-loving plants

7 Gravel surrounding *Monstera deliciosa*

A roomful of greenery, like a clearing in a jungle, is created by this mass of potted plants, including tree ferns, and heart-leaved *Alocasia* next to the door. The contrasting shapes and shades bring the whole veranda to life. To the right of the brick arch is a cedar (*Cedrus deodara*), permanently in place. This would need replacing every 5–8 years, as it outgrew the veranda, but could easily be transplanted to the garden beyond.

● Grouping lots of plants together like this has hidden benefits, apart from their soothing appearance: the air humidity is raised, the effect of drafts lowered, and any damaged parts of the plants can be hidden.

GLOSSARY

Alpine A mountain plant which grows above the tree line and flowers in spring when the snow melts. Gardeners use the term in a broader sense to describe any plant suitable or small enough to grow in a rock garden.

Annual A plant whose life-span—from seed to flowering and death—is less than one year.

Aquatic A plant that grows naturally either completely or partially submerged in water and is decorative in ponds.

Arbor A small-scale garden shelter usually consisting of a timber or trellised frame with plants climbing all over it.

Bedding plants Plants which are planted and displayed for one season only—as opposed to border plants, which are permanent. They may be annuals or biennials or tender plants from the greenhouse.

Biennial A plant that requires two growing seasons to complete its life cycle; for example, a foxglove. Leaves are formed during the first year and flowers and seeds the following season.

Bog plants Plants accustomed to living in permanently wet ground. They have specially adapted roots that can exist on the oxygen in the water.

Borrowed scenery Prospects or views beyond the garden artfully opened up to make the plot seem larger.

Broadleaf Any tree which is not a conifer and therefore has broad rather than needlelike leaves.

Conifer Any cone-bearing tree; also includes yews and junipers which have fleshy fruits. Most conifers are evergreens, with scaly, needlelike or strap-shaped leaves.

Dead-heading Removing faded flowers from a plant, partly for its appearance but also to prevent it from spending its energy on producing seeds. Dead-heading often produces a better crop of flowers the following year; and in the case of annuals, it encourages more flowers in the same year.

Deciduous A plant that loses all its leaves at one time of the year, usually late autumn; the opposite of evergreen.

Dot plants Taller plants "dotted" among shorter ones, used predominantly in formal bedding schemes.

Drift A substantial but natural-looking patch of one plant. For example, daffodils and snowdrops often look best when planted in drifts down grassy banks.

Espalier A lattice-work of wood or wires on which to train trees. Also, a method of training fruit trees, by selecting lateral branches to grow horizontally on each side of the main stem.

Evergreen A plant that keeps its foliage for at least a year. The opposite of deciduous. A wintergreen retains its leaves for one year only.

Exotic Any plant which is not native to the region. In garden design, the word often refers to any plant with big leaves, suggesting a tropical origin, or any feature that looks foreign and out of context.

Fastigiate A variety of tree or shrub with erect branches; eg the Lombardy poplar.

Fern-leaved A description of a deeply and daintily divided leaf of any plant.

Focal point Either an obvious eye-catcher or the point where perspective lines converge.

Foliage plant A plant grown for the sake of its leaves, rather than for its flowers or fruit.

Foundation planting Using plants, such as small conifers or shrubs, to soften the hard lines of a building at ground level.

Gazebo A garden pavilion; strictly speaking, one designed to offer a view.

Glaucous Describes a blue or grey-green leaf or a fruit covered with a waxy film. A grape is a glaucous fruit; a Scots pine needle is a glaucous leaf.

Ground cover Plants used to cover the soil, often between larger plants. They usually provide a dense, weed-proof cover of ornamental foliage that requires little or no maintenance.

Hardy Describes a plant capable of surviving for the whole of its lifespan without any protection from frost. A half-hardy or tender plant may need protection during the coldest months of the year. In hot climates, hardiness may refer to a plant's resistance to drought.

Herbaceous A perennial plant that dies back to ground level each autumn or winter. The term also applies to borders filled largely or entirely with such plants.

Island beds A popular style of planting in beds or irregular curving outlines that can be isolated or grouped in a lawn. Light and air circulation are better than in a border with its back to a hedge or wall.

Knot A formal ornamental flowerbed named for its twisted designs formed with dwarf evergreens.

Marginal A plant that requires a perpetually moist or wet soil and grows best at the edge of a pool.

Patio Almost any terrace or outdoor living area. Originally the inner courtyard of a Spanish house, open to the sky and used as an open-air living room.

Peat garden A bed of peaty soil for growing certain woodland and alpine plants that relish damp and acid conditions.

Perennial A plant that lives for more than two years. Often applied exclusively to herbaceous perennials—plants producing stems that die down every year.

Pergola A walk of pillars and cross-members with plants trained to grow up and over it.

Rambler A plant, especially a rose, that has long, lax stems and is essentially droopy in habit.

Rock garden or **Rockery** A rocky bank, usually artificial, planted with low-growing plants in imitation of a mountain slope. *See also* Alpine.

Rosette The arrangement of plant parts, particulary leaves, into a rose-like form.

Shrub Any plant with many wooded stems, the main ones usually growing from the base.

Specimen plant Any plant (but usually a tree or shrub) grown where it can be viewed from all angles.

Standard A tree with a clear expanse of bare trunk before the head of branches.

Structure The framework of the garden comprising the paths, fences, hedges, the house itself and the permanent planting of trees and shrubs.

Sub-shrub A small perennial plant with woody stem bases and soft tips, which die back every year. The term is often used to describe any small shrub.

Succulent Any plant with fleshy leaves or stem containing juice or sap, adapted to life in arid environments.

Tender Describes any plant likely to be damaged by low temperatures.

Topiary The practice of cutting trees and bushes into ornamental shapes, whether geometrical (balls and cones) or representational (peacocks etc). It has been popular since before Roman times and is now undergoing a revival.

Treillage Trelliswork used to create elaborate screens or architectural structures. This was popular in grand French gardens of the late 17th and 18th centuries.

Trellis A latticework timber screen, used to add height to a wall or, placed against a wall, to support climbers.

Trompe l'oeil A deliberate trick of the eye—eg the use of false perspective effects to make a garden seem longer.

Variegated Applied to leaves and sometimes petals that are marked, spotted or otherwise decoratively patterned with a contrasting color.

Weeping A tree or a shrub of pendulous habit, either natural as in some species of *Salix*, or artifically induced as in weeping standard roses.

Zonal A plant part with a region, often ring-like, of a different color from the remainder. For example, zonal pelargoniums have rings of darker or lighter color on their leaves.

USEFUL ADDRESSES

MAGAZINES

Useful information can be found in the articles—as well as the advertising—of the following publications:

Horticulture
Subscription Department
P.O. Box 51455
Boulder, CO 80321-1455
A slick well-written monthly.

Garden Design
P.O. Box 836
Peterborough, NH 03458
Published quarterly by the American Society of Landscape Architects. Very handsome, with a landscape-architecture slant and many advertisements for garden furniture and ornaments.

Flower and Garden
Circulation Department
4251 Pennsylvania Ave.
Kansas City, MO 64111
Useful bimonthly covering vegetables as well as flowers.

The Avant Gardener
P.O. Box 489
New York, NY 10028
A monthly horticultural newsletter full of up-to-the-minute information. Their once-a-year list of plant suppliers is a treasure.

The Combined Rose List
Beverly R. Dobson
215 Harriman Rd
Irvington, NY 10533
An indispensable complete list of rose varieties available in the U.S. and Europe, with their suppliers.

PLANT, SEED AND BULB SUPPLIERS

These are a few of the best of the national suppliers of plants. Most of the magazines above carry advertising for more plant sources. The *Avant Gardener* list gives virtually all the sources in the United States.

Antique Rose Emporium
Route 5, Box 143
Brenham, TX 77833
Old-type roses. Catalog.

Vernon Barnes & Son Nursery
P.O. Box 250
McMinnville, TN 37110
General nursery stock. Free catalog.

Kurt Bluemel
2740 Greene Lane
Baldwin, MD 21013
(301) 557-7229
Ornamental grasses. Catalog.

Bluestone Perennials, Inc.
7211 Middle Road
Madison, OH 44057
(216) 428-7535
Tiny, inexpensive plants of a large selection of perennials and shrubs. A wonderful way to start a border without spending a fortune.

Breck's
6523 North Galena Road
Peoria, Il 61632
Bulbs—free catalog.

W. Atlee Burpee Company
21774 Burpee Building
Warminster, PA 18974
Seeds, bulbs, plants, tools from America's leading seed company. Free catalog.

Busse Gardens
635 East 7th St
Cokato, MN 55321
Perennials and iris. Catalog.

Carlson's Gardens
Box 305
South Salem, NY 10590
Azaleas and rhododendrons. Catalog.

Carroll Gardens
Box 310
Westminister, MD 21157
General nursery stock. Catalog.

Catalog of Unusual Succulents
553 Buena Creek Rd
San Marcos, CA 92069
(619) 744-8191
Color catalog of varied desert plants.

Cooley's Gardens
11553 Silverton Rd, NE
P.O. Box 126
Silverton, OR 97381
Iris. Catalog.

Daystar Nurseries
RFD 2, Box 40
Litchfield, ME 04350
Perennials. Catalog.

P. de Jager & Sons
Box 100
Brewster, NY 10509
Bulbs. Free catalog.

Dutch Gardens, Inc
P.O. Box 200
Adelphia, NJ 07710
(201) 780-2713
Inexpensive source for good bulbs, some perennials and begonias, gladioli, etc.

High Altitude Gardens
P.O. Box 4238
Ketchum, ID 83340
Alpines. Catalog.

High Country Rosarium
1717 Downing St
Denver, CO 80218
Old and rare roses. Free catalog.

Holbrook Farm & Nursery
Route 2, Box 223
Fletcher, NC 28732
Perennials, bulbs. Catalog.

Jackson & Perkins Co.
Box 1028
Medford, OR 97501
General nursery stock. Free catalog.

Klehm Nursery
Route 5, Box 197
South Barrington, IL 60010
(312) 551-3715
Hosta, iris, peonies and day lilies. Catalog.

Lilypons Water Gardens
P.O. Box 10
Lilypons, MD 21717
(301) 874-5133
Equipment and plants for water and bog gardens. Catalog.

Logee's Greenhouses
55 North St
Danielson, CT 06239
Begonias, ferns, herbs, perennials. Catalog.

McClure & Zimmerman
1422 West Thorndale
Chicago, IL 60660
(312) 989-0557
Large selection of rare and botanical bulbs, a few plants.

Paradise Water Gardens
64 May St
Whitman, MA 02382
Plants, equipment, books on water gardening. Catalog.

Park Seed Co.
Cokesbury Rd
Greenwood, SC 29647–0001
(803) 223-7333
Seeds, bulbs, some plants and tools.
  Free catalog.

Powell's Gardens
Route 3, Box 21
Princeton, NC 27569
Perennials. Catalog.

Rex Bulb Farms
Box 774
Port Townsend, WA 98368
Lilies. Catalog.

Rocknoll Nursery
9210 U.S. 50
Hillsboro, OH 45133
Perennials. Catalog.

Roses of Yesterday and Today
802 Brown's Valley Rd
Watsonville, CA 95076
(408) 724-3537
Old-fashioned and species roses, shrubs
  and climbers, as well as selected
  modern roses. Catalog.

John Scheepers, Inc.
63 Wall St
New York, NY 10005
Bulbs. Free catalog.

Siskiyou Rare Plant Nursery
2825 Cummings Rd
Medford, OR 97501
Perennials, trees and shrubs. Catalog.

Slocum Water Gardens
1101 Cypress Gardens Rd
Winter Haven, FL 33880
Water lilies and goldfish. Catalog.

Stern's Nurseries
Geneva, NY 14456
General nursery stock. Catalog.

Stokes Seeds
Box 548
Buffalo, NY 14240
Seeds. Free catalog.

Thompson & Morgan
P.O. Box 1308
Jackson, NJ 08527
(800) 367-7333
Seeds.

TyTy Plantation
Box 2000
TyTy, GA 31795
Tender bulbs for summer or greenhouse
  growing. Catalog.

Van Bourgondien Bros.
Box A
Babylon, NY 11702
Bulbs. Free catalog.

Vick's Wildgardens
Box 115
Gladwyne, PA 19035
Nursery-grown wildflowers. Catalog.

André Viette Farm & Nursery
Route 1, Box 16
Fishersville, VA 22939
Perennials. Catalog.

Wayside Gardens
Hodges, SC 29695–0001
(800) 845-1124
Perennials, shrubs and trees—large
  catalog of fine varieties.

White Flower Farm
Litchfield, CT 06759–0050
(203) 496-1661
Perennials, bulbs and shrubs described
  in a most informative catalog.

FURNITURE, ORNAMENT AND SUPPLIES

Ballard Designs
2148–J Hills Ave.
Atlanta, GA 30318
(404) 351-5099
Cement garden ornaments, small
  fountains and capitals suitable for
  table bases.

Cassidy Brothers Forge Inc.
US Route 1
Rowley
MA 01969–1796
(617) 948-7611
Ironwork, good traditional designs.

Charleston Battery Bench Inc.
191 King Street
Charleston
SC 29401
(803) 722-3842
Cast-iron and timber benches.

**Chattahoochee Makers
  Company**
1098 Huff Road NW
Atlanta
GA 30318
(404) 351-7016
Hardwood furniture and planters.

Clapper's
1125 Washington Street
West Newton
MA 02165
(617) 244-7909
General suppliers, English teak
  furniture.

Country Casual
17317 Germantown Rd
Germantown, MD 20874–2999
(301) 540-0040
Teak garden furniture.

Dalton Gazebos
7260–68 Oakley St
Philadelphia
PA 19111
(215) 342-9804
Red cedarwood gazebos, good
  trelliswork.

Foster, Kevill
5102 Weststate St
Westminister
CA 92683
(714) 894-2013
Timber planters, traditional.

Garden Iron
116 North Clifton Ave.
Louisville
KY 40206
Garden ironwork, interesting frames
  for climbers in pots.

Gardener's Eden
P.O. Box 7307
San Francisco, CA 94120–7307
(415) 421-4242
Furniture, tools and ornaments.

Gardener's Supply
128 Intervale Road
Burlington, VT 05401
(802) 863-1700
Tools, greenhouses, safe organic pest
  controls.

Gargoyles Ltd
512 S. Third St
Philadelphia
PA 19147
(215) 629-1700
Reproduction furniture.

International Terra Cotta Inc.
690 North Robertson Blvd
Los Angeles
CA 90069–5088
(213) 657-3752
General garden ornament.

Iron Fence Co.
PO Box 467
Auburn
IN 46706
(219) 925-4264
Iron fences.

The Kinsman Company
River Rd
Point Pleasant,
PA 18950
(215) 297-5613
Garden shredders, compost bins and other tools. Free information package.

Lynch, Kenneth & Sons, Inc.
P.O. Box 488
Wilton
CT 06897–0488
(203) 762-8363
General ornament, restoration advice.

Machin Designs (USA) Inc.
557 Danbury Rd
Wilton
CT 06897
(203) 834-9566
Conservatories.

Mrs McGregor's Garden Shop
4801 First St N.
Arlington, VA 22203
(703) 528-8773
Teak planters and other garden gifts. Free catalog.

Mellinger's
2382 DA Range Rd
North Lima, OH 44452
Nursery supplies. Free catalog.

Moultrie Manufacturing Company
P.O. Drawer 1179
Moultrie, GA 31776–1179
(800) 841-8674; in Georgia (912) 985-1312
Iron fencework, furniture and ornaments.

Nampara Gardens
2004 Golf Course Road
Bayside
CA 95524
(707) 822-5744
Redwood garden furniture.

Walt Nicke
Box 667
Hudson, NY 12534
Garden tools and useful ornaments, mostly imported from England. Free catalog.

Park Place
2251 Wisconsin Ave., NW
Washington DC 20007
(202) 342-6294
Showroom for many fine garden furniture lines. Write or call for information.

Robinson Iron
Robinson Rd
Alexander City
AL 35010
(205) 329-8486
Cast-iron work, traditional

Skagit Gardens
1695 Johnson Rd
Mount Vernon, WA 98273
Professional and recreational horticultural tools and supplies. Catalog.

Smith and Hawken
25 Corte Madera
Mill Valley
CA 94941
(415) 383-4415
General suppliers, importing from the UK.

Vintage Gazebos
Dept. 367
513 S. Adams
Fredericksburg, TX 78624
(512) 997-9513
Pre-assembled gazebos and Victorian fretwork. Catalog.

Walpole Woodworkers
767 East St
Walpole, MA 02081
(617) 668-2800
Many different styles of wooden fences, as well as attractive garden buildings and furniture.

Winterthur Gift and Garden Sampler
Winterthur Museum
Winterthur, DE 19735
(800) 848-2929
Classic reproduction planters and ornaments, as well as some choice plants.

Wood Classics Inc.
RD 1, Box 455E
High Falls
NY 12440
(914) 687-7288
Timber furniture.

INDEX

PICTURE CREDITS

Photographic sources are listed in roman type; owners/designers are named in *italics*.
Abbreviations: T top; B bottom; C centre; L left; R right.

Title and half-title pages: Linda Burgess
Contents TL: Cynthia Woodyard
Contents CL: *Oehme, van Sweden & Associates, Inc.*
Contents BL: Linda Burgess
Contents TR: Heather Angel
Contents CR: John Heseltine
Contents BR: Jerry Harpur/Owner-designer *Marion Pedder*
8: Linda Burgess
9T: Jerry Harpur/Owner-designer *Marion Pedder*
9B: Linda Burgess
10T/B: Linda Burgess
11T: S. & O. Mathews/*Martin Furniss's garden at Cobblers*
11B: Henk Dijkman/The Garden Picture Library/ Designer: *Henk Weijers*
12T: Ron Sutherland/The Garden Picture Library
12B: Liz Gibbons/Natural Image
13T: John Glover
13B: Henk Dijkman/The Garden Picture Library/ Designer: *Henk Weijers*
15TL: Ron Sutherland/The Garden Picture Library
15BL: Linda Burgess
15TR: David H. Russell/Designer: *Myles Challis*
15CR: Uli Butz
15BR: John Heseltine
16: Linda Burgess
17: *Oehme, van Sweden & Associates, Inc.*
19: John Neubauer/Designer: *Oehme, van Sweden & Associates, Inc.*
23: Ron Sutherland/The Garden Picture Library
26L: *Oehme, van Sweden & Associates, Inc.*
28R, 29L/R, 30, 31TL/BL/R: Jacqui Hurst
32R/TL, 33TR/BR: John Heseltine
35L/R: Liz Gibbons/Natural Image
36L, 37LR: The Harry Smith Horticultural Photo Collection
39: Nicky Gibbs
40R, 41: Jerry Harpur/Designer: *John Vellam*
43TL/TR/B: Jerry Harpur/*Derek Nimmo*
45L/R: Clifton Nurseries/Photos: Clive Corless/Designer: *Victor Shanley*
47, 48BL/R, 49: Jerry Harpur/Designer: *Mackenzie Bell*
51L/R: Ianthe Ruthven
52L/53: Tania Midgley
54R, 55L/TR/BR: Heather Angel/*Private garden, Wales*

56L, 57L/TR/BR Tania Midgley
58L, 59TR/BR: John Heseltine
60R, 61: Bob Gibbons
62L, 63L/R: Tania Midgley
64R, 65, 66L/R. 67L/R: John Neubauer/Designer: *Oehme, van Sweden & Associates, Inc.*
69L/TR/BR: Jerry Harpur/Designer: *Victor Shanley*
70L, 71: Harry Smith Horticultural Photo. Collection
72R, 73L/R: Jerry Harpur/Designer: *Brophy, St Albans*
75L/R: Kenneth Scowen
76, 77L/R, 78L, 79: John Heseltine
80TR/BR, 81: Ron Sutherland/The Garden Picture Library
82L, 83L/R: Cynthia Woodyard
85TL/TR/B: John Heseltine
86BL, 87: Jerry Harpur/Designer: *Peter Rogers*
88R, 89, 90R/TR/BR, 91: Margaret Turner/Garden and Landscape Pictures
92R: John Neubauer/*Oehme, van Sweden and Associates, Inc.*
93L: *Oehme, van Sweden & Assoc, Inc.*
93R: John Neubauer/*Oehme, van Sweden and Associates, Inc.*
94R, 95TL/BL/R: Jerry Harpur/Designer: *Hillier and Hilton*
97L/R, 98B, 99L/R: John Heseltine
101: Harry Smith Horticultural Photo Collection
102R: John Heseltine
103: Heather Angel
105TL/TR/B: Jerry Harpur/Designer: *Rodney Slatford*
106T/B. 107: Jerry Harpur/Designer: *John Brookes*
109, 110TL/BL/R, 111: Cynthia Woodyard
112L, 113R: Nicky Gibbs
114R, 115L/R: John Neubauer/*Oehme, van Sweden and Associates, Inc.*
117TL/BL/R: Jerry Harpur/Designer: *Geoff Kaye*
118BR, 119L/R: Michelle Garrett
121L/R: Harry Smith Horticultural Photo. Collection/ Designer: *Jean Bishop*
122B, 123L/R: Tania Midgeley
124R, 125, 126, 127L/R: Cynthia Woodyard
129L/TR/BR: Jerry Harpur/Designer: *Michael Blood*
130L: *Oehme, van Sweden & Associates, Inc.*
131, 132L: John Neubauer/Designer: *Oehme, van Sweden & Associates, Inc.*
132: *Oehme, van Sweden & Associates, Inc.*
133: John Neubauer/Designer: *Oehme, van Sweden & Associates, Inc.*
134R, 135L/TR/BR: Heather Angel/Owner/designer: *Freda and Joe Brown, Leeds, Yorks.*
136, 137: Good Housekeeping/Photo: Marianne Majerus/

Designers: *Caroline Boisset, George Carter, Raf Fulcher, Elizabeth Tate*
139, 140L/R, 141L/R Ianthe Ruthven/Designer: *Arabella Lennox-Boyd*
142TR/BR, 143, 144TL/TR/B, 145: Cynthia Woodyard
147: Henk Dijkman/The Garden Picture Library/ Designer: *Anthony Paul*
148L/R, 149: Ron Sutherland/The Garden Picture Library/Designer: *Anthony Paul*
150TR/BR, 151: Linda Burgess
152R, 153: Ron Sutherland/The Garden Picture Library
154: Ron Sutherland/The Garden Picture Library/ Designer: *Anthony Paul & John Duane*
155: Ron Sutherland/The Garden Picture Library/ Designer: *Anthony Paul*
156TR: Steve Wooster/The Garden Picture Library/ Designer: *Merrist Wood Agric. College, Chelsea Flower Show 1987*
156BR, 157: Steve Wooster/The Garden Picture Library
158B, 159: Ron Sutherland/The Garden Picture Library

The author and publishers would like to thank the numerous garden owners and professional designers who have co-operated, directly or indirectly, in the making of this book – not only those listed above but also those whose names could not be traced. It is hoped that the photographs themselves are an ample testimony to their various talents and tastes.